Whitework Quilting

Karen McTavish

Whitework Quilting

Creative Techniques for Designing Wholecloth and Adding Trapunto to Your Quilts

Karen McTavish

On~Word Bound Books
innovative publishing

Two Harbors, Minnesota

Whitework Quilting Copyright © 2004 by Karen McTavish

The information in this book is presented in good faith, but the challenge of photographing white quilts is monumental. The publishers of this book encourage the reader to view the quilts in person, if at all possible, as their portrayal here is limited by size and technology.

Greatful acknowledgement is made to Scholastic Inc. for granting permission to reprint copyrighted material from MORE QUILTS FROM THE QUILTMAKERS GIFT 2 by Joanne Larson Line. Published by Orchard Books/Scholastic Inc. Copyright © 2003 by Joanne Larson Line. Reprinted by permission.

Editor's note: Four quilts featured in this book were not available for studio shots. We photographed the quilts on-location and used the same two-page spread format as the rest of the quilts.

Published by On-Word Bound Books LLC. / 7004 Olson Road / Two Harbors, Minnesota 55616

http:/www.onwordboundbooks.com/

Library of Congress Cataloging-in-Publication Data

McTavish, Karen C.
  Whitework quilting : creative techniques for designing wholecloth and adding trapunto / by Karen McTavish
      p. cm.
ISBN 0-9744706-0-0
1. Trapunto--Patterns. 2. Machine quilting--Patterns. I. Title.
 TT835 M478 2004
746.46--dc22
                              2003025901

Printed in the United States of America

10 9 8 7 6 5 4 3 2 1

❧ *Dedication*

*T*o my beautiful, talented, and patient daughter, Allison. You are the very best part of me.

Table of Contents

🌿 *Introduction* 🌿

*O*nce upon a time, a longarm machine quilter had placed her award-winning, machine quilted, white trapunto/wholecloth in a quilt show. As quilters sometimes do, she anonymously "hung out" by her quilt, hoping to overhear comments from the unsuspecting passersby (come on, you do it too!) She chalked this up to educating herself on what to do better next time. The viewers critiqued her quilt out loud, unaware that she was standing behind them. The machine quilter was silently glowing, proud of her wholecloth's blue ribbons for best category and best machine-quilting. Her smile lit up the room; she was beaming from ear to ear. If a car had then hit her, God forbid, she felt that her work on earth was now done. She had completed her life's journey with this; her wholecloth, trapunto masterpiece. Life was good.

She listened pensively, her head reeling from the positive reactions of fellow quilters as they passed by her quilt. "Oh, look at that white, hand quilted wholecloth!" and "...all that work!! Can you imagine??" Like most machine quilters, she focused on the negative rather than the positive, and her machine quilter's bubble burst and pride crumbled away as she heard those fateful words:

> "Oh, its machine quilted...
> ...never mind."

The viewer walked away. Was the quilt now marked by the kiss of death? The message seemed to be: It is not okay for a machine quilter to be doing whitework quilting. Only hand quilters need apply.

My life changed from there. I was determined to make machine quilting as respectable as hand quilting. I would combine machine quilting with wholecloth and trapunto. There are no rules here, are there? Where is the Quilt-God? Did she lay down the law, and no one filled me in on the rules? Since acceptance is the key to happiness, my decision was to create machine quilted, wholecloth quilts that would no longer be viewed as unacceptable. Machine quilting became my conscious choice as the tool to use in creating these historic masterpieces.

Wholecloth quilts are major attention-getters. They do very well in quilt shows. Wholecloth/ Trapunto quilts are commonly chosen for "Best Machine Quilting" awards. They are so beautiful and impressive that they seem intimidating. Most of my students are amazed at the wholecloth quilts they are able to design, add trapunto to, and quilt. Many a student wholecloth has brought a tear to my eye.

To me, whitework quilting suggests a plain piece of fabric in great need of heavy, fabulous quilting to bring the unadorned space out of the ordinary and into a soul-satisfying conclusion. I like to pull up a chair, sit, and lovingly gawk at a wholecloth, turning my head this way and that, fully absorbing its beauty. I can't explain the impact that wholecloth and trapunto quilts have on me. Perhaps it could be similar to when a person happens upon a certain type of rare sports car, immediately stops, turns around to look closely at the car, and a dream-like stare comes over them. I am similarly mesmerized by wholecloth; it takes my breath away. This book is the outcome of my passionate addiction to wholecloth and trapunto quilting.

The most common question I hear from my wholecloth students is, "How long did that take to machine quilt?" My reaction is always the same. I think, "Does time really matter? Did the hand quilter log her hours with dread and depression?" She very well may have, but I like to think she was having such a good time that she only dreaded the time she was away from her quilting project. Trapunto and wholecloth are truly a labor of love but the rewards are great and numerous. I can imagine what the historic hand quilter went through, and I feel grateful for her service. When I think that a wholecloth quilt only takes me about 60 hours to design, trapunto, quilt, and bind vs. 3000 hours of hand quilting, I am absolutely humbled.

When I teach wholecloth workshops, you may hear me say, "What would a hand quilter do?" When I feel stuck or in doubt about my design, knowing a hand quilter has done the hardest stencil or quilting pattern in her masterpiece, helps me to make a good choice of design in mine. I can usually go into denial about the hours of effort it's going to take and focus on the end result instead; this artistic style of whitework takes a rock-solid time commitment to see the project through to completion.

Although the quilts in this book have been created using longarm quilting machines, the designing process and techniques for adding trapunto to any quilt (pieced, appliqué, or wholecloth) are just as applicable to the use of other sewing machines or hand quilting.

Trapunto is widely used in today's quilting. Unfortunately, the English and French heirloom wholecloths are a dying tradition.

We need to reach back and take hold of them. Today, with the use of longarm and domestic quilting machines, we are able to complete these masterpiece quilts in a timely fashion while making them strong and durable.

I want to bring this traditional style of quilting into the 21st century and emphasize the hours of labor involved in trapunto, wholecloth and whitework quilting. I want machine quilting to be respected, to be an acceptable way to pass down a quilter's artistic talents from generation to generation. Hopefully this book will inspire you to create your own masterpiece quilt by reaching into history and bringing forward the lost art of wholecloth and whitework quilting. 🎕

🐚 *Architectural Inspiration* 🐚

When I am working on a wholecloth, I like to get visual inspiration from architectural aspects found around my home town of Duluth, Minnesota. You will most likely have historic buildings and remarkable homes in a city near you too. As you drive around you can get great quilting ideas from older buildings, churches, museums, Victorian homes, fences and iron works without leaving the comforts of your car.

I am always looking for new ideas that appear traditional but are still new and exciting in the quilting world. I find inspiration from front doors to furniture. I often find myself sitting in front of some random building or taking photos of a tombstone. Generally, this is for reasons which only relate to designing my wholecloth.

Sometimes, when I suddenly become quiet in the car, my daughter will say, "You're thinking about a quilt design, aren't you!?" Busted! When I am hit with an epiphany, the birth of my next wholecloth is only guaranteed if I can jot down the design on a piece of paper before I forget what it looks like. A camera would also be nice to have on hand in this situation. Of course, it never is.

I sit in my car and stare at a design on a structure and wonder how I can incorporate it into a wholecloth quilt. I think about how hard it would be to achieve the design work in stone or wood. I figure that if beautiful scrollwork can be created in those mediums, then I can attempt it using fabric and thread.

Gathering Ideas for Inspiration

*T*his ironwork door also has a fabulous house attached to it – but it's the ironwork I love. It inspires a desire to quilt beautiful and intricate scrollwork in my wholecloth quilts.

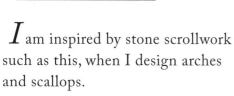

I am inspired by stone scrollwork such as this, when I design arches and scallops.

*T*his beautiful archway is one of my favorite places. You may find me sitting in front of this building, waiting for inspiration to strike.

*H*ere, found above a doorway, is an example of what could be an intricate border motif for a wholecloth quilt. As I drive around town, I take pictures of architectural objects to inspire quilting ideas, to avoid creative burnout, and to keep thinking outside the box.

*S*ometimes I see woodwork - furniture, archways, picture frames - that has beautiful scrollwork carvings and I am completely inspired to reproduce the design in a wholecloth.

*T*his fabulous ceiling at the Fairlawn Mansion and Museum simply takes my breath away. It is screaming for someone to convert its design into a quilt.

"Passageway" (40" x 49")

*This original wholecloth/trapunto with adapted designs was quilted on my longarm quilting machine. The inspiration for my quilt comes from my love of design and texture. The architectural motifs remind me of grace and beauty. _____ I combined the designs to remind me of what may lie _____ in heaven, along with a reminder of the beauty that my _____ own city has within itself, everywhere I look. This quilt has taken many blue ribbons, and will eventually become part of the Benton County Historical Museum's collection. Wholecloth and trapunto are techniques that I cherish and specialize in. – **Linda J. Alexander, Oregon Machine Quilting Company***

Linda's quilt is a direct result of her love of architectural scrollwork. She was open to creating a wholecloth without the traditional use of feathers and the result is stunning. The center motifs, corners, and frame were marked directly on the wholecloth. Linda's choice to use radiating lines throughout her wholecloth proved very effective in drawing the eye inward. Linda also uses historic information in her quilt which is traditional in wholecloth design. This gives interest to the quilt as well as respecting the past. This quilt does very well in shows because the designs are original and the piece is well balanced; a combination which makes this quilt worthy of a museum retirement.

"Venetian Lace" (83" x 83")

This original wholecloth design was inspired by love of Italian architecture. Its curves, formal structure, depth and detail are so pleasing to me. I wanted this quilt to have a harder feel, a stone or marble like appearance, yet not be simple or stark. Although I am drawn to the soft warm look of feathers, I challenged myself to use an unusual theme. My intention was for this quilt to be different from the others I have seen in quilt shows. The main designs of this quilt came from two books by Helen Squire. I transferred designs from her books onto paper and then to my quilt top.
– Melanie Austin, Huckleberry Stitches Custom Machine Quilting

*M*elanie's award winning wholecloth uses architecture and nicely packed trapunto which highlights all the scrollwork in her quilt. Melanie came to class with Helen Squire's books and was ready to start marking her wholecloth immediately! She could see that the current trend in wholecloth was "going scrollwork" and wanted to challenge herself to design a wholecloth using only architectural inspiration. Helen Squire's book, *Helen's Guide to Quilting in the 21st Century © 1996*, had several different options for Melanie's design plan. During class, Sherry Rogers and Melanie worked for many hours marking this quilt top. The border design was a bit challenging to nudge together, but in the end it came together flawlessly.

"Class with Karen McTavish" (38" x 38")

I have always been interested in wholecloth quilts; the design and stitching speak for themselves. When I had the chance to take Karen's wholecloth workshop, I jumped at it! It turned out that the design of the quilt, not the execution, was the most taxing part of the workshop for me. The fun part with this quilt was that after I decided what I wanted to do, I had to figure out how to use a rectangular design as the center medallion of a square quilt. Answer: modify the stencil and turn it into a square. As you can see, it worked, and I am very pleased with the whole experience.
– Kathryn Blais, Quilted Treasures

*K*athryn's wall hanging was challenging from the beginning. She really loved a rectangular stencil but wanted a square wall hanging. She modified the stencil as we marked it to the fabric. She also added smaller motifs as fillers into her centerpiece from other stencils in my stash. Her feather border had two different directions of travel and had to meet at four points. The hill and valley of the feather border adds a subtlety which softens the "bump" where the feathers meet in the center and does not distract from the overall effect of the quilt.

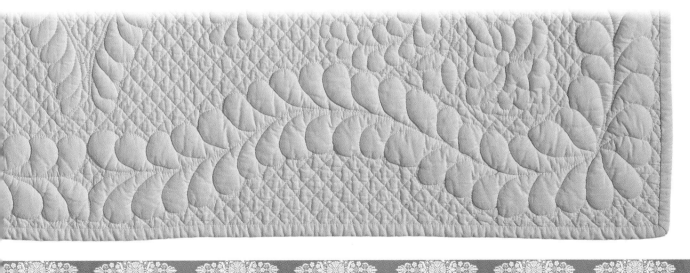

"Bountiful Harvest" (56" x 68")

This original wholecloth quilt started in a workshop with Karen McTavish. The center design was taken from an 1800's Baltimore Brides appliqué pattern which was rotated and repeated four times. This was my first attempt at trapunto and was created during my first year machine quilting. – Janiece Cline, Piece by Piece Quilting

Janiece came to class with a stack of out of print, paper appliqué patterns, which I had never seen before. Each appliqué design was very traditional and could have been used as a centerpiece in her wholecloth, repeated or alone. Janiece picked the most difficult one to use in her wholecloth – the dreaded grapes! I found a grape and vine stencil in my stash, a perfect match for her border. We were very impressed with ourselves for our creative minds. I heard Janiece ask, "How long do you think this is going to take to trim away all this batting?" I pretended another student needed my help and ignored her question. The grapes in her centerpiece and border required Janiece to cut away the batting from each individual grape. Remember - points are not given for level of difficulty but I still hold her in the highest regard for completing her wholecloth. Micro-stippling was the only option as a background grid to make the individual grapes pop out. The feather frame adds a nice touch around the center design. Janiece's quilt appears to have cording in her border vines; it is actually closely cut trapunto. No short cuts were taken with this quilt and for her first wholecloth – it is breathtaking.

"Beauty in Brown" (48" x 48")

*T*his wholecloth is quilted with light brown thread instead of white. The brown thread is used in the motif areas only. The background quilting is in white thread which matches the fabric. This old hand quilting trick results in stronger and more noticeable motifs. The low-loft, poly batting used in the trapunto designs did not have enough loft to show off the motifs, but the brown quilting thread does the trick! The undulating feather border, which circles the center design, was hand drawn on the quilt using modified stencils to achieve the desired design. I do not recommend this much stippling in a quilt as judges find it a little boring. This quilt took a 3rd place ribbon in a national quilt show.

–**Karen McTavish**

"WEDDING CHUPPAH" (58" x 66")

In some traditions the Chuppah, or wedding canopy, is passed down from mother to first-born daughter. It symbolizes the new home the couple will establish and also signifies God's blessing of the marriage. The Chuppah is supported by four long poles, held by groomsmen, one at each corner of the quilt. When the bride arrives at the Chuppah she circles the waiting groom seven times with her mother and future mother-in-law, while the groom continues to pray. This symbolizes the woman as a protective, surrounding light of the household, illuminating it with understanding and love from within, and protecting it from outside harm. The number seven parallels the seven days of creation and symbolizes the "new world" the bride and groom are about to create. The original stencil design is "McScrollwork" and the fabric is a poly-satin (used for wedding dresses) found in a 60 inch width. Thank you to my sister, Jennifer, and her new husband, Lowell, for allowing me the excuse to quilt my first Chuppah for their beautiful wedding.

– *Karen McTavish*

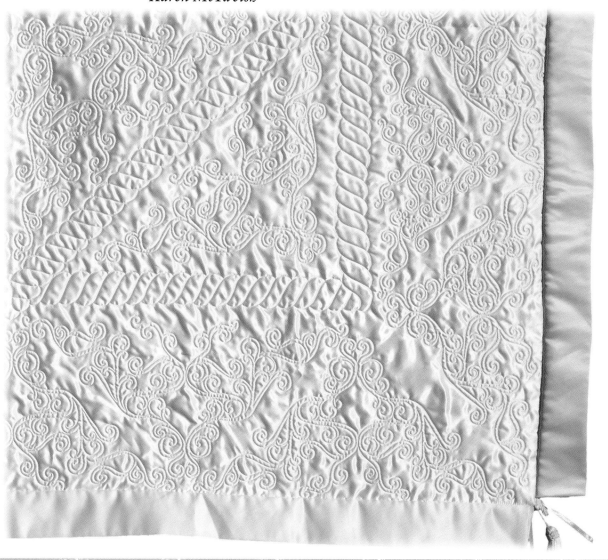

"Silver Threads" (40" x 40")

$\mathcal{T}$he idea for "Silver Threads" came from the silver anniversary theme of the Minnesota State Quilt Show. As the title of the quilt indicates, the machine quilting thread used was all silver metallic. The original fabric was a wide, sheer, batiste fabric with black velvet placed between the layers, which produced the grey shadow under the trapunto (shadow trapunto). My mother

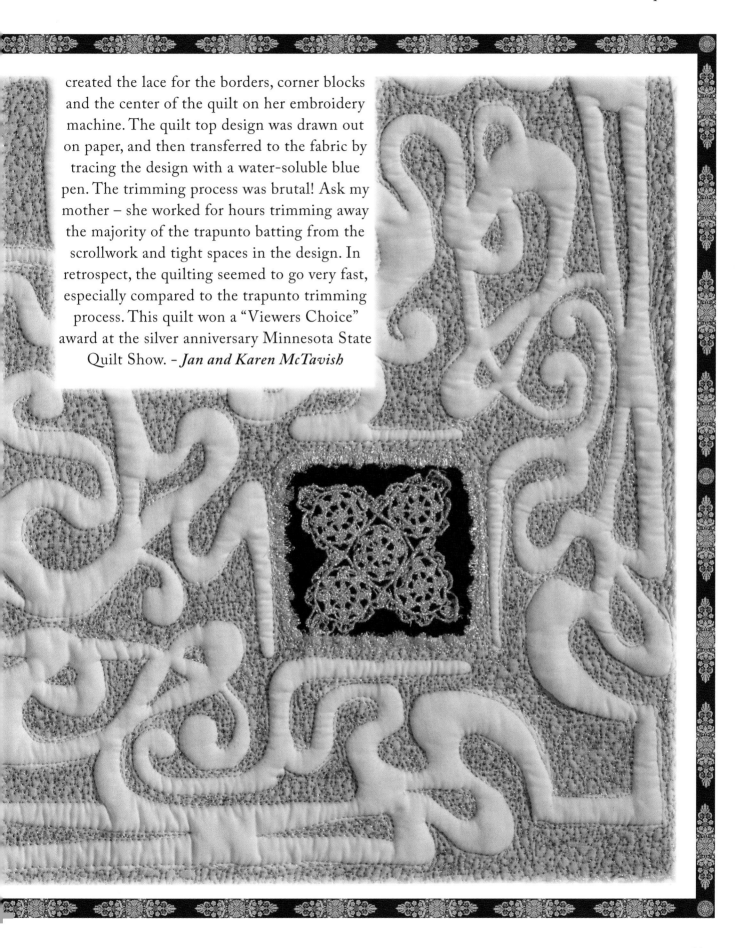

created the lace for the borders, corner blocks and the center of the quilt on her embroidery machine. The quilt top design was drawn out on paper, and then transferred to the fabric by tracing the design with a water-soluble blue pen. The trimming process was brutal! Ask my mother – she worked for hours trimming away the majority of the trapunto batting from the scrollwork and tight spaces in the design. In retrospect, the quilting seemed to go very fast, especially compared to the trapunto trimming process. This quilt won a "Viewers Choice" award at the silver anniversary Minnesota State Quilt Show. - *Jan and Karen McTavish*

"WHITEWORK LONG AGO" (84" x 94")

*T*his wholecloth was made for my father. I was rushing to finish this quilt before a show deadline and he helped carpool my daughter to and from school for a week. He also helps me with all my bookkeeping. This whitework is a thank you from his grateful daughter. Since wholecloth historically incorporates information in the quilt, I put my father's initials, DGM, and the year, 2002, in the center. This original, trapunto wholecloth was designed mostly on paper and then transferred to the fabric. The batting is washable wool. Wool has a long memory and this batting remembers my fold lines! In the rush to finish this quilt before the show deadline I was forced to take a shortcut - a grim decision; I did not trapunto the center of the quilt or the borders. The designs cannot be seen well because the main batting is so flat. When the quilting critique came back it said, "Quilter should have trapuntoed the center and the borders". This quilt won an "Honorable Mention" award in a national quilt show.

– Karen McTavish

"Psalm 127" (39 ½" x 34 ¾")

*"Psalm 127" is a wholecloth rendering of our home, started in a class with Karen McTavish. I brought an enlarged photograph of our house and used the light box technique to directly mark the material. The color trapunto was accomplished with bright felts and flannels placed under sheer lawn fabric. The complimentary threads help to bring out the shades of the trapunto. This wall hanging celebrates 25 years of family life in our home. It is a special addition to my growing collection of custom, memory quilts. - **Marcia Rhone, Clear Pond Quilting**

*T*his is an excellent example of using different colors of felts, fabrics and flannels to achieve the "color trapunto" technique. When Marcia told me her idea in a private workshop, I was thrilled. This wholecloth, wall hanging has a very contemporary design to it. It takes us away from wholecloth/ whitework history and puts us in the 21st century of quilt making. This is a very personal piece of work; it is literally the home of the quilter from an enlarged photo. The color adds so much interest to the piece that it looks painted.

"A Whole New World" (38 ½" x 50")

While designing my first wholecloth quilt, I knew I wanted to incorporate trapunto, feathers, curves and ovals. I bravely tackled the ¼ inch, diagonal lines and micro-stippling on my longarm quilting machine. The top and backing are unbleached muslin with matching quilting thread. I used a very high-loft, poly batting to enhance my trapunto. My wholecloth was created in a workshop taught by Karen McTavish and Sherry Rogers when they were teaching as a wholecloth team. This quilt opened the door to a new world for me.
Janice L. Walsh, Cat's Meow Quilting

*T*his quilt is special to Janice but also special to me, because of a wonderful drafting tip my father taught me. Without this advice, the very large feather oval would not have been possible for this quilt. Cut a piece of twine or string twice the length you want your oval to be. Tie the ends together in a tight knot. Place a tack on your quilt top at both the highest and lowest points of the intended oval and wrap the string around both tacks leaving some slack in the line. Measure the string placement to make sure it is in the center of the quilting design. Place a blue, water-soluble pen inside the loop of string and push the pen to the side until the string is tight against the pen. Run your pen around the inside of the string, allowing the string to create a natural curve, and soon you will have a custom oval marked on your quilt top. Add feathers to the oval and it becomes a one of a kind, hand made design.

Supplies, Materials, Tools & Equipment

$\mathcal{H}$ere are some of the tools you will need to
create your own trapunto/wholecloth quilt.

*H*ere are some samples directly from my white, cone thread stash. I use lots of weights and types of threads. In general, the most important thread issues for machine quilters are avoiding breakage and noticeable starts and stops. One of the most common critiques I see is, "watch your starts and stops". I want thread that allows me to get away with a few mistakes and makes my stitches look their very best.

*T*here are several different water-soluble threads available on the market, but for industrial longarm machines, I recommend the 1,500-yard cone of "Vanish". It is the only product that my machine can handle without breaking. You might have to loosen your tension slightly; it is very lightweight thread. The thread is a **warm** water-soluble product. **Cold** water will not vanish the "Vanish"! Also, avoid licking your fingers when threading your needle (I always love that!)

*T*he bobbin thread needs to match the color of the quilt top. Quilting the trapunto batting is a temporary process. We use the bobbin thread and the "Vanish" as we would a glue stick or duct tape; it's just holding our batting in place until we dunk the quilt in water. The "Vanish" goes away forever but the bobbin thread will "float" inside the quilt for the rest of its life - hopefully unseen.

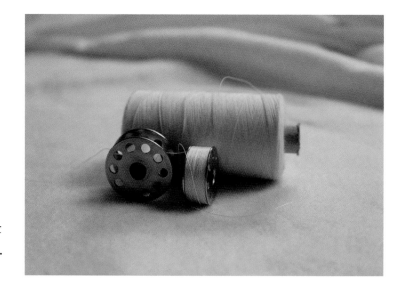

I need to go to "Stencil Anonymous" because I have a stencil addiction. When I go to quilt shows I make sure to have a budget that allows me to buy a ton of stencils. I am currently going for architectural as well as traditional, hand-quilter style stencils. I love them! No continuous line stencils for me please. I've developed some techniques for longarm quilters which eliminate the need for continuous line stencils. These are detailed in my book, *Quilting for Show*. I try to buy stencils on the large side. I've noticed that almost all my quilting has some sort of stencil use. I have come to rely on stencils and have no fear of using them.

I really like to draw my own designs on paper. In most quilt shows, originality will be well rewarded. You will need large paper sheets, preferably with a one inch grid, pencils, permanent black markers, and a source of inspiration - such as the ironwork on someone's front door.

*W*hen working with white quilts you might notice a black snippit of thread that somehow got quilted into your quilt - much to your horror. To remove these random noticeable threads, I use a tiny little crochet hook to pull that rascal out by maneuvering through the weave of the fabric. If you can see something in your quilt, then a judge can too.

*B*lue Mark B Gone Water-Soluble Pens (not "fine-point") are best for marking wholecloth quilts and light fabrics on pieced quilt tops. The quilt will need to be submerged in water after quilting to avoid clouding or ink reappearance. Spraying water on the markings may not remove the product completely. You may just push the blue into the batting and backing, where it may still be visible. To avoid recurring marks, completely submerge your quilt in a tub of water (such as your washing machine). Spin gently and dry your quilt flat.

I would not attempt a wholecloth quilt without several Clover Eraser Pens at the ready. I remember the days when I would have to spray a marking mistake with water, and then wait hours until the fabric dried so I could re-mark it. The water would spread and the wholecloth would be cloudy with blue pen marks. The Clover Eraser Pen gives me the ability to take out a mistake with minimal pain and agony. Some eraser pens leave a yellow color when used with a pink water-soluble pen, so I only use the Clover pens with blue water-soluble pens and purple disappearing ink pens.

*T*he Purple Air-Erasable Pen (disappearing ink, not "fine-point") is great for fabrics which cannot be washed or allowed to get wet. This pen is not desirable for trapunto or wholecloth. The markings will have disappeared within 24 hours or sooner depending on humidity.

*B*ruynzeel Chalk Pencil in color #886 is a pastel artist's chalk pencil which I found in a local art supply store. I have tried many different products for marking on dark fabric and this pencil seems to do the best job in my experience. It's easily removable on dark fabric, has no waxy ingredient, gives me a nice fine point using a standard pencil sharpener and generally doesn't break off while using it with plastic stencils.

Straight edges and drafting tools can be very helpful for measuring and marking registration lines during the wholecloth design process. I like to use rulers to create background fillers and grids.

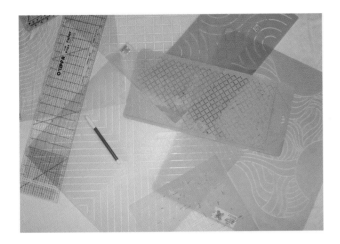

I also buy background stencils to use as auditions, so I can see what the grid will look like next to my designs.

Dangerously pointy scissors make a better looking, sculptured trapunto which resembles appliqué. I won't lie to you; they are weapons which can cause serious damage to your quilt during the trapunto trimming stage. Some scissors have blunt noses, but that doesn't mean you won't snip your quilt top. On the contrary; you may compensate for not having a nice point by curving your scissors and the results are the same: a snip in the fabric. If this is your first attempt at trapunto, you are likely to snip your quilt top. I suggest a sacrificial, practice quilt, willing to take many snips if need be, to improve your trimming ability. Once you have a few trapunto quilts under your belt, you will rarely nick the fabric. It's all about practice.

*P*oly batting with a loft of 12-20 oz. is best for traditional trapunto. I like to use a 16 oz. poly for my trapunto batting. The thickness is just right; I don't have to raise my hopping foot to quilt over the batting and the loft is noticeably different than the main body of the quilt. 20 oz. batting can be very dense and may require several snips of the scissors just to get through the layer. Some battings look thick, but if they are not dense, they will reduce down to nothing and appear flat. Sometimes a dense, flat batting is desirable for shadow trapunto where loft is not always needed.

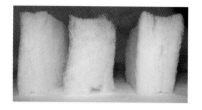

*B*atiks are a great choice for designing a shadow trapunto quilt. The neon bright fabrics will appear pastel when placed between the layers of the quilt - if the quilt top is translucent or semi translucent. Pre-wash these colorful fabrics to avoid bleeding.

*A*crylic felt, which can be purchased at any retail fabric store, can be found in 60 inch widths. The brighter the color you choose, the better the trapunto result. Acrylic felt will not shrink or bleed and it is as easy to trim away as traditional trapunto batting. It can be used for shadow trapunto too – see Sue Schmieden's quilt.

*G*enerally, wholecloth quilts are white or off-white. If the main batting of the quilt is dirty with seeds or bits of twigs as seen here, brown spots will appear on your quilt top and backing after soaking the quilt to remove the blue pen marks and water-soluble thread. Removing these spots can be difficult but can be done after several washings. I am careful to insure that my batting is clean.

🦋 *Wholecloth* 🦋

My mother said, "We are going on a road trip." Our destination was Kalona, Iowa, near the boyhood home of my father, his parents, and my grandparents - a place of many happy childhood memories. We were two machine quilters about to advance on a tiny Amish town with its many quilt shops and exquisite hand quilters. This was where wholecloth started for me.

At the time of this road trip I was feeling creatively empty. I had been machine quilting for some time but wanted something more. Looking back, I don't think I knew I was ready to move on to more advanced quilting, but I knew I was bored and needed something more exciting in my quilting career.

Knowing how to be a respectful Minnesotan, I walked carefully and quietly into the first quilt shop with my mother, my hands at my sides. It was a countryside barn that had been converted into a large quilt shop. When I opened the door I saw a group of women sitting around a wholecloth quilt on a hand quilting frame. The blood drained from my head and suddenly I could hear the entire score from *West Side Story*. I asked my mom if she heard any show tunes and she said I needed to get my hearing checked.

I had tunnel vision. All I could see was the half-quilted wholecloth. The experience

seemed almost spiritual. With my heart in my throat and nodding my head in the respectful "walk-by-nod-mode" perfected by many years in Minnesota, I moved on past the women hoping they wouldn't find out that I was their nemesis – a machine quilter. In reality, they didn't even look up from their work. I noticed they were in the zone - the wholecloth zone. Where's my zone? I want a zone! Did I have a zone?

I was just a customer in a quilt shop and

was not about to break their concentration by screaming my excitement at the top of my lungs, finger-snapping and leap-frogging over my mother's shoulders to land with a thud proclaiming I was going to quilt like that someday! What they were doing was completely awesome. I wanted to ask them to move over, please, so I could give it a go. I wanted to be in that quilting circle - to become one of them.

I tip-toed around the women and finally one of the gals looked up at me. I froze. How does one manage to show honor, respect and awe in a single glance? I hoped she could look into my eyes and pass all her knowledge to me via eye beam. Since nothing new in terms of wholecloth knowledge seemed to appear in my mind, I continued on my silent, respectful search for the meaning of wholecloth. Maybe the secret is working without electricity. Although willing to give it a go, working by candlelight is not really an option. I wouldn't be able to turn on my quilting machine! This would be a major problem.

The women were using plastic stencils for quilting designs and marking them with a graphite pencil. I knew that the value of their hand quilted, wholecloth quilt would be much higher if the marks were still visible upon completion. This would not apply to me. A machine quilter must not have visible marking lines on her quilt.

I decided I would need a stencil stash of monstrous proportions. Like a quilter who must buy more and more fabric without knowing why, I became a quilting-stencil junkie. In every quilt shop I would find and buy all the new stencils that I could get my hands on. My main quilting supplies would be stencils, water-soluble pens, and wide fabric. If I die with the most quilting stencils, it is because of the Amish women in Kalona, Iowa.

I looked at my mother and she looked at me. It was time to go on to the next quilt shop. While my mother brought her 47 bolts of fabric to the cutting table, I inched closer to the group of women around the wholecloth. If I hadn't attended so many rock concerts in my younger years, I may have been able to make out what they were talking about (the tricks of the trade and all the years of experience they had) but no, I couldn't hear a thing.

As we were leaving the quilt shop all I could manage to get out of my mouth was a softly mumbled and greatly understated, "It's so beautiful." The women looked up and one gave me a warm smile and said…. "Thank You." ✂

A Brief History of Wholecloth

Some of the first signs of wholecloth quilting date as far back as 3000 B.C. to Egypt, India, Iran, China, and other places in the Orient. However, most of what we know today about the four traditional types of wholecloth quilts comes from the influential traditions of the Amish, English, Welsh, and French. This book primarily focuses on the English variety of trapunto whitework.

Wholecloth quilts were (and still are) considered to be the "Masterpiece Quilt" in a quilter's life. They were made for dowries and handed down through the generations. A hand-quilted, whitework-trapunto wholecloth could take up to 3000 hours to complete. In England, during the 16th century, Queen Elizabeth had a small army of needle workers. She enjoyed giving white wholecloth quilts to her royal guests.

To create an exquisite piece (especially by hand) a quilter would have needed a passion on the same lines as a compulsion or addiction with a large dash of creative drive, full-blown commitment, and clean working space. Perhaps the incentive for such passion came from the heart of a single woman in the market for a husband. Young women were expected to be accomplished in their quilting abilities, and a whitework wholecloth quilt may have been equivalent to the modern practice of placing a large personal ad in the classifieds. In my experience, this old world calling card of the single female looking for a husband doesn't work in the modern era.

I have read that the makers of wholecloth quilts were usually "women of leisure". To me, this conjures up an image of a quilter, stretched out on her fainting couch, eating bon-bons. Completely bored out of her mind, she moves over to her quilting frame and adds a few stitches here and there to pass the time. The leisure quilter generally came from a wealthy family. They could afford the extravagance of large pieces of fabric in silk, glazed wool, and cotton special-ordered from the Orient. After waiting 4-6 months for the wholecloth fabric to arrive by ship I'm sure the quilt had a good chance of completion, especially since the well-off could afford to hire needle workers to quilt to order. Petticoats and gowns worn under and over great skirts frequently displayed wholecloth style quilting. Gowns were extremely heavy. Often the front of the gown was cut away to show off beautiful quilting and embroidery on the petticoats.

Elegant wholecloth quilts were popular with prosperous Americans too. In 18th century New England, whitework wholecloth quilts were worth nearly six times the value of most household inventories. It is not surprising that people in the country thriftily pieced quilts, while people in the city favored wholecloth and whitework quilts.

In less wealthy families, shared beds were common. A four-poster bed with a quilt that hung to the floor could accommodate at least 4 people. Without running water, bathing was a luxury. Heavy perfumes were often used to cover odors and the quilt tended to get quite soiled, which I am sure is an understatement. When the quilt was stained beyond recognition or repair, it was usually dyed yellow – a color that covered most stains. When a dyed quilt could no longer be used as a bed covering, it was used as a mattress pad. It is not surprising that antique wholecloth quilts are seldom seen.

For those who could not afford large pieces of fabric but wanted to make a wholecloth-style quilt, a top could be pieced together with any fabric available, including recycled clothing scraps, until it became the desired size. The fabrics were different shades of white with oddly placed seams all over the quilt. The backing would have been pieced from 3-4 looms worth of linen. Sometimes linen thread was used for quilting.

In the late 18th century, cloth was still comparatively expensive and quilts were valuable possessions. However, in the early 19th century, the Industrial Revolution made textiles more abundant and less expensive. Today, wide-width fabrics are fairly inexpensive and are no longer assumed to be a sign of wealth. Throughout the 18th and 19th centuries, whitework wholecloth quilting was widely admired and respected. I think we can say this still holds true today.

Some of the common tools used for designs were teacup saucers, paper drawings, dinner plates, etc. Most quilters used a pencil lead to draw the designs for whitework. Amish quilters continue to use this method to this day.

Rose Kretsinger - an American quilter, jewelry designer and artist, became known world wide for her appliquéd quilts in the mid 20th century. Her hand-drawn, paper quilting designs were regularly handed down to her friends in quilting groups and guilds - a way for women to mentor others and keep the quilting tradition alive.

Traditional wholecloth reflects the 19th century revival of Greco-Roman motifs such as scrolling feathers with wide borders, grapes, medallions with frames, and intricate designs to pull your eye inward. A newer trend is to use architecture to inspire your designs and leave plenty of "white-space" for cross-hatching or radiating and diagonal straight-line quilting backgrounds. This allows the quilting designs to have a higher relief, so the motifs are the main focus.

Today, wholecloth quilts are never pieced, and traditionally do not include any color other than white, off white, or yellow. Machine stippling is not a traditional background filler but still works for the wholecloth quilt if it is very small and tight and resembles lace. Wholecloth quilting does not have blocks or rows; it appears as a framed portrait of elegant quilting. Fabric selection for today's wholecloth could be cotton, linen, muslin, wool, cotton sateen, batiste, or any fabric in wider widths. Creating a modern wholecloth quilt is still a labor of love. It is a commitment, whether quilting by machine or hand.

Wholecloth has had different names throughout the centuries. You may have seen these terms and wondered what they meant:

"Counterpane" refers to any wholecloth which does not have batting. This style of quilting is extremely rare today. Counterpanes were always pieced together in white or off-white with closely matching pieces of fabric. Some counterpane quilts incorporated trapunto. Counterpane and trapunto quilts started to appear in colonial America around the 1600's. The wholecloth quilt remained popular in Wales (in particular) and kept the tradition of highly decorated wholecloth quilts alive throughout the early 1900's.

The "Linsey-Woolsey" wholecloth quilt uses one side of linen (the backing) and the other side wool (the top). Wool was abundant in America and Britain from the 1750's through the 1820's and well known for warmth. Popular from the 1750's to the 1850's, this style of quilt was very large (up to 3 or 4 loom widths) and was pieced together. The quilting designs of these quilts were extremely large and exaggerated. The quilting ranged from simple diamond grids to elaborate curvilinear feathering, formed into borders, flowers, wreathes, and plumes very similar to whitework quilting. These quilts were very heavy and must have been difficult to quilt and mark.

A finer version of linsey-woolsey is the "Calimanco" spread. The woolen fabric was finished to a high shine by rubbing the wool with a smooth stone until it took on a gloss, or by coating the fabric with a mixture of egg whites and water to create a shiny glaze. In the 1820's the wool cloth was commercially heat pressed to give it an overall sheen. During the late 1700's, American quilters imported Calimanco fabrics to use for their quilt tops. Calimanco was also used in quilts made by professional English needle workers. The quilting designs included vines, shells, and feathers of gigantic proportions. Examples of Calimanco and Lindsey-Woolsey quilts are seldom found today.

The elegant white on white, or "Whitework",

quilt was very popular in the 1800's and reached its peak in 1860 in New England. Traditionally, these quilts had a linen backing with a white cotton top. Usually, both the top and backing were pieced. If batting was used it was a thin layer of finely combed wool or cotton. It was more common to have no batting at all. The designs on the plain white material were achieved entirely by intricate quilting. The best needle workers demanded that the top and the backing be virtually indistinguishable and that the average eye be unable to see where the backing had been seamed. The classic design was a central medallion: a cornucopia, a latticed basket of fruit, an eagle, a pineapple, or a feather wreath surrounded by a border of grapevines, trailing leaves, or swags. Customary motifs of feathers, wandering vines, leaves, flowers, fruits and trees were used in addition to figural designs including ships, animals and people. Dates and names were also included in the quilting designs. The terms "feather", "feathering" and "princess feather" came from the ostrich feathers worn in ladies hats from this era. Whitework (white cotton, linen, silk, etc.) was a status symbol. It was elaborate, romantic, dramatic, fancy and bold. 🦋

Fabric Selection

*C*hoosing your wholecloth fabric depends on the style of trapunto you will be doing. If you want to achieve shadow or color trapunto you will need a semi-translucent or translucent fabric. Go ahead and audition thin fabrics to sheer fabrics. Batiste is good, but any sheer fabric will do. I always check to see if I can see

through the fabric before I purchase it. If you do not want to add color to your wholecloth and would like a plain white fabric, I would choose a good quality cotton fabric of a wide width. Using cotton fabric for your wholecloth, such as cotton-sateen, will give your quilt a long lasting life. There are many different wide fabrics to be found in your local quilt shops. Your choice of fabric should be based on color, sheen, transparency, and durability. You want a quality fabric as your wholecloth will become a family heirloom to treasure for many generations.

*T*here is a wrong side and a right side to all fabrics. To find the right side of the fabric, look and feel for the smoothest side. By placing the fabric on your knee, you can see the weave in the fabric very clearly. When I can see the weave, I know that is the wrong side of the fabric. It's important to use the right side of the fabric because the wrong side tends to "pill" up, like a well worn sweater, after you have completed your wholecloth. Use your gut instinct to help you choose the right side.

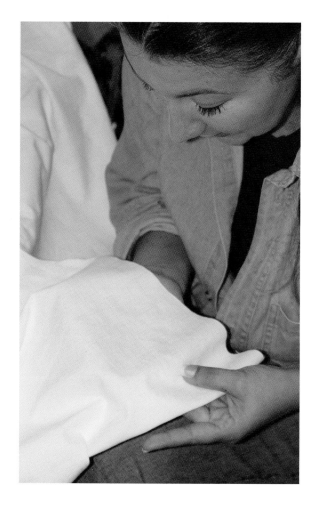

Cutting and Squaring - Up

When you wash and press your fabrics for your wholecloth, don't be surprised if you end up with an irregular looking piece of fabric such as this. It's important to square up the fabric so it will hang and lay flat. This means that each side of the fabric should be the same length. The edges should not appear wavy or ragged. The edges of the fabric are sometimes used as guides for your background fillers, so it's important for them to be straight. Also, your fabric will not hang straight if it was ripped on the grain. You may see a pull in the weave towards an edge of the fabric.

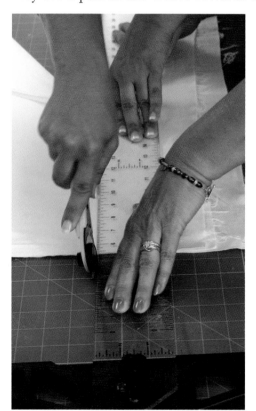

I like to use drafting tools like T-bars, long rotary cutting rulers and measuring tape to figure out the dimensions of the quilt top. A good rule to keep in mind is that plastic stencils are designed to work best with even numbers. Remember that when designing a quilt top and you will have much less "nudging" to do.

After insuring the fabric is trimmed straight, you will need to decide how big you want your finished wholecloth to be. You may want to add up to 1 inch extra all the way around for pinning and binding space. It's important to plan for your finished wholecloth be an even size. This example shows the finished dimension will be 46 inches but it will be cut at 47 inches to give some playing around room. I find the extra space helpful but not critical.

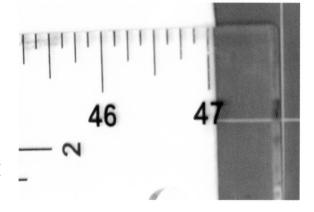

Registration Lines

*A*fter cutting and squaring up, I have straight edges for my wholecloth fabric. The edges are my guideline for the first marking of the quilt. I use a blue, water-soluble pen to mark the finished dimension on the edge of the fabric (¼ to 1 inch away from the fabric edge). This line will be my guide for any straight-line or crosshatching background filler.

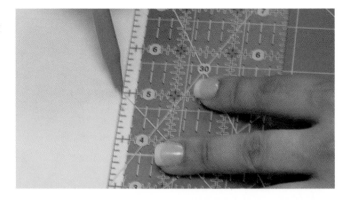

*T*he wholecloth is now ready for registration lines. Find the center of the quilt by folding the fabric into fourths (quarters). Pinch the fabric with your fingers where the center point will be and then open up the quilt again. You will see a "plus sign" in your fold lines. Mark the "plus sign" with your blue, water-soluble pen as shown. Also mark the center or mid-point of each side of the quilt top.

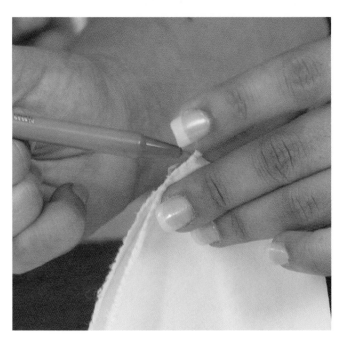

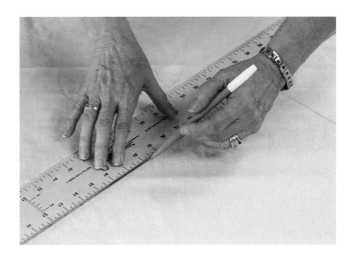

$\mathcal{D}$raw diagonal, vertical and horizontal registration lines with your blue water-soluble pen, as shown. You will need a long ruler, or you can butt several rulers up next to each other to get the desired length. Having plenty of table space is very helpful for this step.

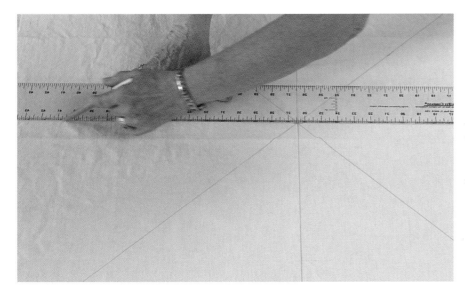

$\mathcal{U}$se the reference marks you made in the center and on the edges of your wholecloth in the previous step to line up your ruler. If you squared up your fabric correctly, all of your lines should bisect your center "plus sign".

$\mathcal{A}$fter marking all of your registration lines, your quilt top should look like this. You are now ready to start auditioning stencils and planning your design.

Auditioning Stencils and Marking Your Designs

*N*ow it's time to pick out stencils for your wholecloth. It's fun to go through your entire stencil stash every once in a while, isn't it? It's okay to be clueless about what to do with that wholecloth in front of you. When choosing a design it's important to know that you can let it come together as you go. I start with either a centerpiece or a border. This is determined by how much I like a design. If I really like a border stencil I start marking that design first. But, if I pick out a centerpiece that I really love, then I start by marking the wholecloth with the medallion. The rest of the quilt will come together. The trickiest part of designing your wholecloth quilt is knowing when to stop! You might find yourself filling in every available space with quilting designs. Remember to leave some plain areas or whitespace for background fillers, such as crosshatching. I like to walk away from my quilt every so often to get the overall effect. When I put some distance between myself and my quilt, I can see what it needs and what it doesn't need.

*P*lop a stencil down in the center of the quilt to see if it looks good on point or in a square setting. Look through the stencil to line up your registration lines with the stencil design.

I like the "no-math method" of wholecloth design. All you need are registration lines to place your stencil. I do a lot of plopping and sliding. I slide the stencil until the edges of the stencil motif are just touching the registration lines as seen here. I can audition the stencil in many different ways. If I place the edge of the stencil on my registration lines I can mark the design on the fabric to create an enclosed frame. Having separated design areas gives me the opportunity to change my background fillers several times throughout the quilt.

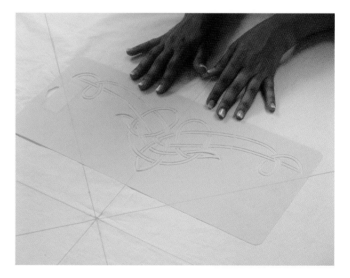

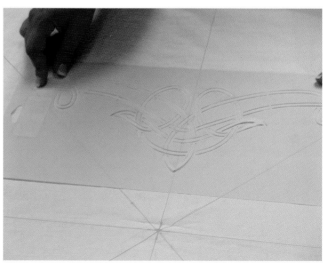

*H*ere is another example of "plop and slide." You can plop down your stencil and slide it towards the middle of the quilt. When the stencil design hits the registration lines center it, adjust it, mark it and repeat it until it connects all the way around and makes your frame.

*T*his is a cool design for a couple of reasons. First, when trapunto is added, it's going to look like cording. Also, Celtic knot work is a classic hand quilting motif. The machine quilter can now handle just about any hand quilting stencil on the market. It just takes determination to find the path to make the design continuous. This is also an excellent example of using the "no-math method." The stencil was auditioned to make sure it would fit the fabric. Luckily, there was no major "nudging" to make the border design touch.

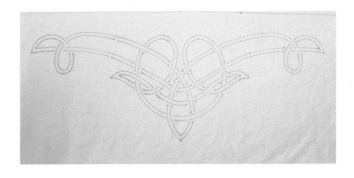

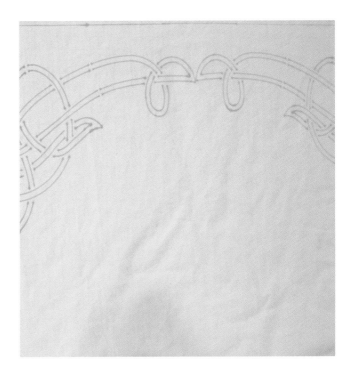

$\mathcal{N}$ow that the center and border designs have been marked on the wholecloth, it's time to audition additional fillers and framers. Before you do this, you may want to walk away from your wholecloth and look at it from afar. This will help you get a feeling for formal proportions and give you a push in the right direction for additional motifs.

$\mathcal{T}$he center, center frame, and borders have been drawn in. This wholecloth is ready for its background fillers.

$\mathcal{I}$t's good to have several different background stencils on hand to help generate ideas. Playing around with the stencils can help you decide on 45 degree angles or ½ inch crosshatching. Keep in mind that your background fillers need to be fairly heavy when you are using trapunto.

You can use a light box to design your wholecloth. This works great when you have a drawing or photo that you want to trace onto the fabric. You may have to enlarge your photo and print it out. See Marcia Rhone's quilt (pages 30-31).

"WHITE PANSY WHOLECLOTH" (69" x 69")

This quilt is a product of a wholecloth workshop given by Karen McTavish. I never thought I would be interested in doing a wholecloth quilt; I took the class only because a friend wanted me to take the class with her. Now, I have two more wholecloth quilts started and others in the idea stage. Creating this wholecloth changed my approach to quilting in general and has taken the mystery out of trapunto. The fabric is high quality bleached muslin, with 16 oz. trapunto batting and 80/20 cotton batting as the main batting for the quilt. – Teddy Wicktor Ahern

*T*eddy is one of those amazing students who seemed fearlessly ready to take on a project of large size. She had been longarm machine quilting for over 4 years when I met her and was unafraid to use traditional hand quilting stencils. She picked the *Rose Kretsinger Scroll*; a paper design set under the wholecloth and traced onto the quilt top. The scroll was set as a frame for the feathered center medallion, and cross-hatching was used as background filler. Micro-stippling used around the borders produced the desired effect of high relief in the trapunto. The complicated border, which is similar to scrollwork, has corners which mirror each other. Although the border stencil Teddy used is very difficult to join, she was able to get the borders to "nudge" together with great success! The *Rose Kretsinger Scroll* can be found in a wonderful book called *Fine Feathers*, by Fons and Porter.

"FLOWERS IN THE CLOUDS" (58 ½" x 58 ½")

This quilt was started during a workshop I took with Karen McTavish. It is my first attempt at designing and quilting a wholecloth from scratch. The feather scallop in the center of the quilt was designed by repeating one portion of a cable and feather border stencil. It was placed next to the registration lines which surrounded the center medallion. The flower clusters were slightly altered from the original stencil to make the design fit in my center wreath. Quilting and finishing this wholecloth was both fun and a great experience. This quilt has won several awards including Best Machine Quilting. – Jill L. Bennett, Quilter with a View

$\mathcal{J}$ill's wholecloth was really fun to design with her. I showed Jill how to draw scallops - a great framing element in a quilt - and off she went. She was able to audition her centers and corners until she found an eye-pleasing combination. Jill and I agreed that flowers go well with feathers; and that flowers in a wholecloth quilt seem to be favorable to judges at quilt shows. The radiating lines throughout the quilt proved to be backbreaking work. Jill had to bend over the quilt with a long T-bar to draw in each line one at a time. I believe Jill finished her masterpiece because she had made such a time commitment already and was determined to get this quilt done. The machine quilting went much faster than the marking. It's a beautiful and classic wholecloth.

"Roses are Red" (94" x 112")

*This was my first customer-commissioned wholecloth quilt. The plain red fabric was sent to me with specifications on what size and shape was needed for the wholecloth, and instructions to be creative. What a fun challenge! And knowing how extremely thrilled my customer is with her new quilt makes this a rewarding experience for me. – **Kathryn Blais, Quilted Treasures***

Wholecloth quilts traditionally allow a pillow tuck and kick pleats in the two bottom corners of the quilt for the posts found on four-poster beds. This was common in the rare, Linsey-Woolsey quilts. Kathryn's customer knew her wholecloth history. Traditionally, the Linsey-Woolsey quilt was linen on one side and brightly dyed wool – with colors such as reds, oranges, pinks, and blues – on the other. Kathryn's red cotton wholecloth is pieced together, top and back. This was the only option as her customer wanted a specific red fabric, which only came in 45" inch widths. In the past, the very large, Linsey-Woolsey quilt was usually pieced together as well - sometimes up to 3-4 loom widths wide! Piecing panels together was the only choice for a large wholecloth before wider width fabrics were commercially obtainable. Today, we have much larger wholecloth quilts as wide fabrics are commonly available in most fabric and quilt shops. A judge may deduct points from a wholecloth which is pieced or historically inaccurate.

"Such Big Plans" (61" x 61")

This wholecloth quilt was a first time experiment for me and didn't quite turn out as planned! I used the "faux trapunto" technique which uses two battings without any cutting or trimming (the top batting is a puffy, poly batting which is layered over a flat, cotton batting). The stencils I used are 19th* century, reproduction designs – heavily modified to fit the intended spaces. The background quilting was done using lightweight, Egyptian-cotton thread, rather than normal quilting thread,*

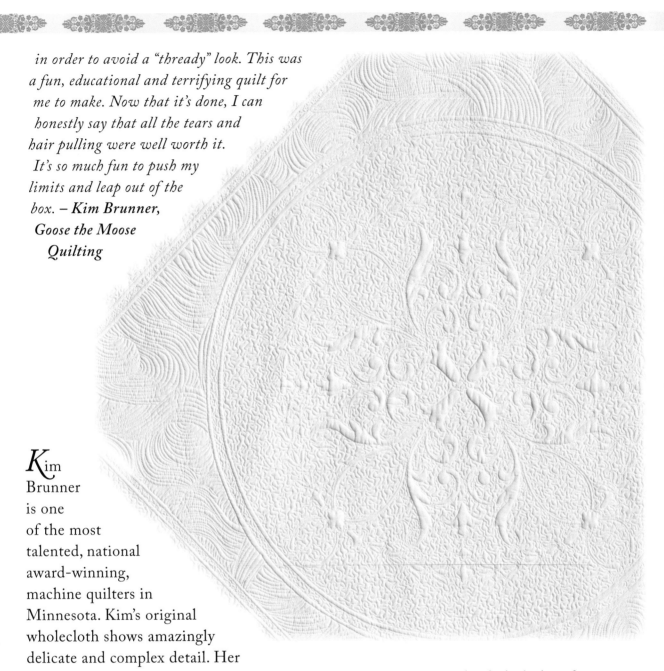

in order to avoid a "thready" look. This was a fun, educational and terrifying quilt for me to make. Now that it's done, I can honestly say that all the tears and hair pulling were well worth it. It's so much fun to push my limits and leap out of the box. – Kim Brunner, Goose the Moose Quilting

*K*im Brunner is one of the most talented, national award-winning, machine quilters in Minnesota. Kim's original wholecloth shows amazingly delicate and complex detail. Her quilt also shows us some very common problems that can arise with wholecloth and trapunto projects. Kim has been kind enough to allow me to use her quilt as an example of some of the nightmares that can happen in the wholecloth world. First, the poly batting she used, coupled with the faux-trapunto technique, did not create enough loft - which makes the quilting designs hard to see. A higher loft and cut-away trapunto (difficult and time-consuming when working with tight, detailed scrollwork) would make the beautiful motifs pop out of the quilt. Secondly, she used a cotton batting which still contained bits of dirt or seeds; after washing the quilt, tiny, brown spots appeared. Kim washed this quilt several times with an oxygen based cleanser and was finally able to remove the stains. Happy Ending.

"Faded Roses" (19 ½" x 19 ½")

This small wholecloth was designed in a class taught by Karen McTavish and quilted on a longarm machine. I wanted to try out some new contrasting threads and decided to add some color to the plain white fabric. I used pale pink thread for the roses and green thread for the leaves. Although the pink thread worked well on the longarm quilting machine, the color was not deep enough. This resulted in my "Faded Roses." - Winnie Haley, Winnies Quilting

*W*innie's wall hanging only took two stencils to design. This small project was perfect for someone willing to attempt trapunto for the first time. This quilt shows what a difference contrasting threads can make on white fabric. Contrasting threads tend to be very unforgiving and it takes a brave person to use them throughout an entire wholecloth. Darker thread on white fabric shows obvious extra stitches, stops and starts; the small mistakes scream out for attention. Matching the thread color to the wholecloth gives you some freedom to make an extra, unintended stitch here or there and not feel the need to rip it out.

"ROSES" (40" x 40")

This one-of-a-kind wholecloth is a direct result of a wholecloth workshop I attended with Karen McTavish. This is my first trapunto project as well as my first wholecloth quilt. I really enjoyed the entire process and was very pleased with the results. Now, I want to quilt another wholecloth!
- Shireen Hattan, Shireenz Stitchez

*T*his off-white wholecloth shows a couple of unique characteristics. Instead of using the classic, off-white thread which would have matched her quilt top, Shireen used a slightly darker, tan thread throughout her quilt. Sometimes, matching thread can give the wholecloth a flat, somewhat "blah" look. Quilting with a darker thread is an old, hand quilting technique used to give extra definition to the motifs. The combination works very well; Shireen's trapunto looks much higher than it really is. Also, notice how the corner fan stencil was used as her centerpiece as well as a border scallop. A one-of-a-kind! Judges tend to enjoy floral designs and the originality of the entire structure will turn a judge's head.

"Southern Sampler" (26" x 26")

I completed this sample project after the class I took with Karen McTavish. I wanted to try trapunto and quilt a small wholecloth. I used a pastel variegated thread for the background stippling to add a hint of color to my wall hanging. **- Carol Hilton, Southern Heritage Quilting**

*C*arol's wall hanging was designed in class and was quilted at her leisure after class. When I first saw the completed quilt, I was amazed that so much color was achieved just by using a pastel variegated thread. The last time I saw Carol's quilt was in the trapunto trimming stage. The difference a little color makes! I will be the first one to admit I am too traditional to use contrasting threads in my wholecloth, so I am showing you Carol's brave and fearless project using variegated thread.

"KATHLEEN RENIE" (86" x 89")

My first attempt at a wholecloth quilt began at a private workshop in Karen McTavish's studio.
I love pansies, feathers and radiating lines so I focused on adding these elements to my wholecloth.
When I have made quilts in the past, I have always thought of the recipient of the quilt. When I
was working on the embellishments of my wholecloth, the one person who kept coming into my mind
was my granddaughter, Breanna Kathleen Renie. With recurring thoughts of her, I chose "Kathleen
Renie" as the title. The quilt will be Breanna's once both my husband and I are gone.
- Kathy Knox, Quilting Memories by Kathy

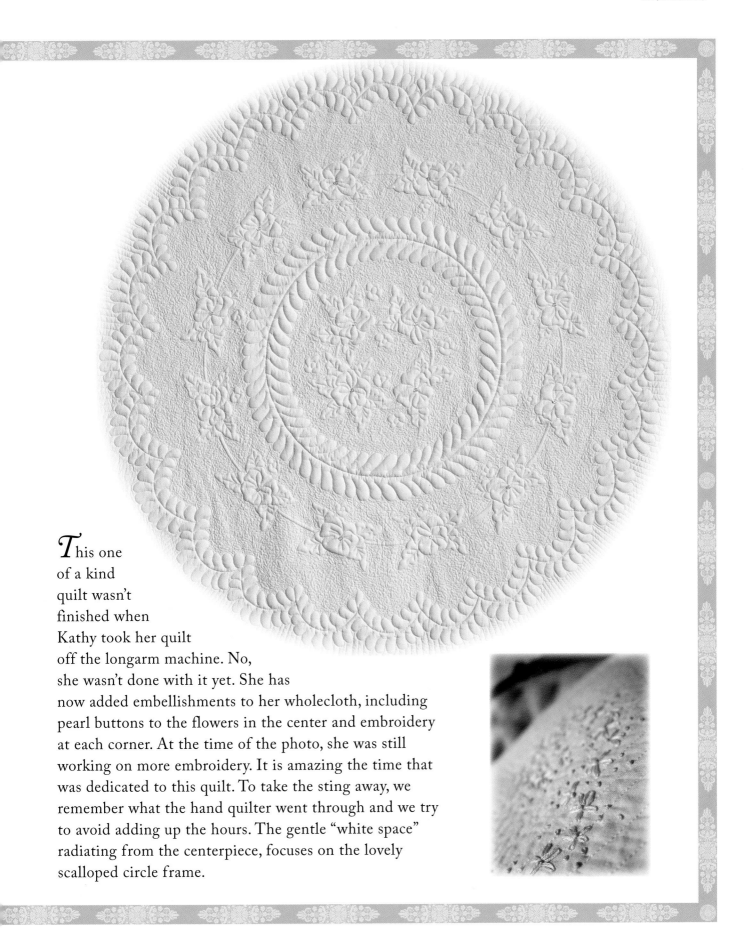

$\mathcal{T}$his one
of a kind
quilt wasn't
finished when
Kathy took her quilt
off the longarm machine. No,
she wasn't done with it yet. She has
now added embellishments to her wholecloth, including
pearl buttons to the flowers in the center and embroidery
at each corner. At the time of the photo, she was still
working on more embroidery. It is amazing the time that
was dedicated to this quilt. To take the sting away, we
remember what the hand quilter went through and we try
to avoid adding up the hours. The gentle "white space"
radiating from the centerpiece, focuses on the lovely
scalloped circle frame.

"WHOLECLOTH AND PATIENCE" (78" x 100")

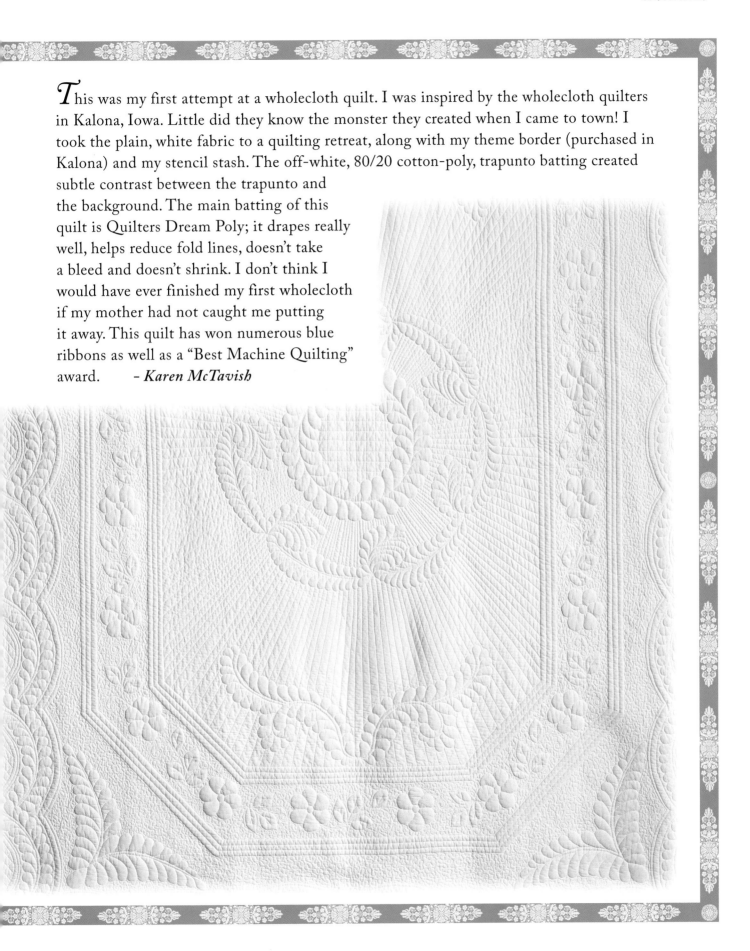

*T*his was my first attempt at a wholecloth quilt. I was inspired by the wholecloth quilters in Kalona, Iowa. Little did they know the monster they created when I came to town! I took the plain, white fabric to a quilting retreat, along with my theme border (purchased in Kalona) and my stencil stash. The off-white, 80/20 cotton-poly, trapunto batting created subtle contrast between the trapunto and the background. The main batting of this quilt is Quilters Dream Poly; it drapes really well, helps reduce fold lines, doesn't take a bleed and doesn't shrink. I don't think I would have ever finished my first wholecloth if my mother had not caught me putting it away. This quilt has won numerous blue ribbons as well as a "Best Machine Quilting" award.   – *Karen McTavish*

"Challenging" (67" x 67")

When attending any quilt show I am always drawn to the wholecloth quilts to admire the wonderful quilting that creates the design. My desire was to design and quilt my own wholecloth. I decided to make a completely white quilt, using trapunto to add to the detail. I used a good quality, cotton fabric with washable wool as my trapunto batting. I did not realize the hours it would take to achieve my goal! I am very satisfied with the results and in 2003 my quilt took a blue ribbon in wholecloth.
- Debra S. Murphy, One Stitch at a Time Quilting

Debra attended a workshop in my studio and was willing to design a large wholecloth. She chose one of the most challenging quilting designs a machine quilter could tackle - Celtic knot work! Hence, the name of the quilt. Debra is a meticulous, machine quilter. She did not hurry her project in any way and took no short cuts. Her background fillers were time consuming, and the design work, complicated. She emailed me several times to inform me of the hours it was taking to trim away her wool trapunto batting, then emailed me again to tell me the hours it took to quilt this amazing quilt. Again, the avoidance of short cuts and time-savers paid off big time. Her quilt is amazing! This wholecloth is completely original and has great overall impact for future judging. Even the publishers of this book were very impressed by this quilt when it arrived for its photo shoot.

"THE GIFT" (60" x 60")

This wholecloth quilt was the result of a workshop with Karen McTavish. I designed it as my class project and it proved more challenging than I expected. Although I did not get to complete the project by the end of the workshop, I did finish it later. I entered it into a national quilt show and won a ribbon in the wholecloth category. While I was thrilled about the ribbon, the real treat was seeing my mother's reaction when I told her the quilt was hers! This is how I came up with the name of the quilt. - Christine M. Olson, Cascade Custom Quilting

*T*his original wholecloth was a challenge for Christine but her hard work and dedication paid off in the end. Her white, wholecloth quilt is a classic heirloom to give to a mother. And what a great gift to receive! Her award-winning work speaks volumes about her wholecloth design ability; but let's get into the flawless construction of the quilt. Christine is very precise when it comes to thread tension, straight line quilting, stitch consistency and starts and stops. These important factors play a big part in any judged quilt.

*"*E*YE* C*ANDY" (42" x 40")*

This fabric was designed by Ricky Tims. When I saw it, there was no doubt in my mind how I was going to quilt it! Amongst my collection of quilting ideas is a coloring book by Ruth Heller. Her design of the "Phoenix," with its feathers wrapping around the artwork, seemed to be perfect for this fabric. I received permission from Ms. Heller to transfer the design to a medium of my choice. Viola, "Eye Candy" was born! For the finishing touch, a Swarovski Crystal found its place in the eye of the Phoenix. – Sherry D. Rogers, Runway Ranch Longarm Quilting Services

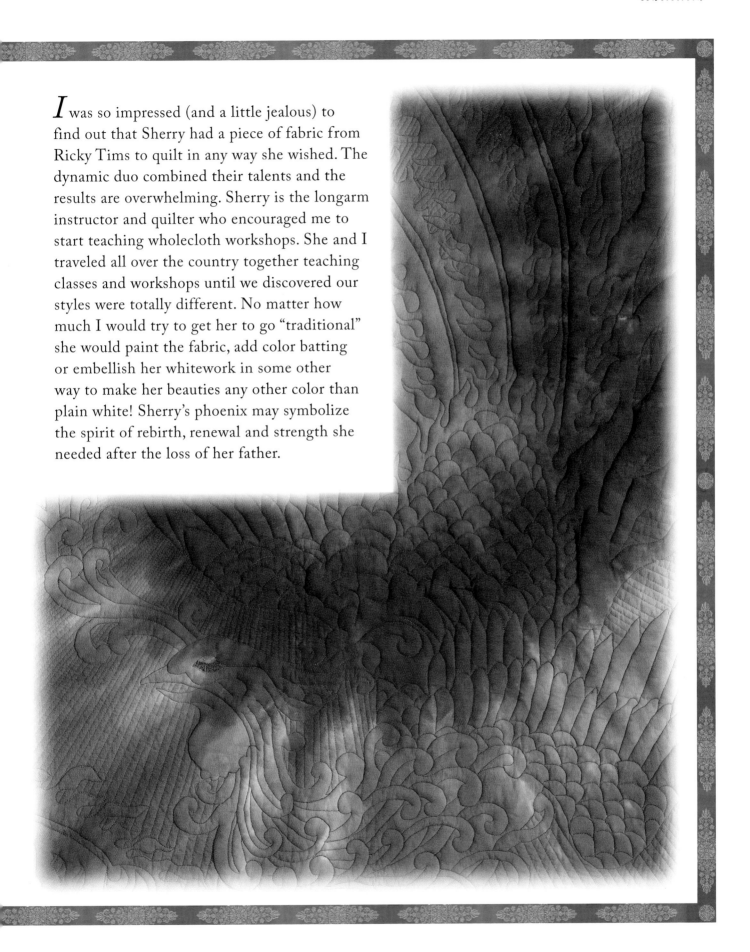

I was so impressed (and a little jealous) to find out that Sherry had a piece of fabric from Ricky Tims to quilt in any way she wished. The dynamic duo combined their talents and the results are overwhelming. Sherry is the longarm instructor and quilter who encouraged me to start teaching wholecloth workshops. She and I traveled all over the country together teaching classes and workshops until we discovered our styles were totally different. No matter how much I would try to get her to go "traditional" she would paint the fabric, add color batting or embellish her whitework in some other way to make her beauties any other color than plain white! Sherry's phoenix may symbolize the spirit of rebirth, renewal and strength she needed after the loss of her father.

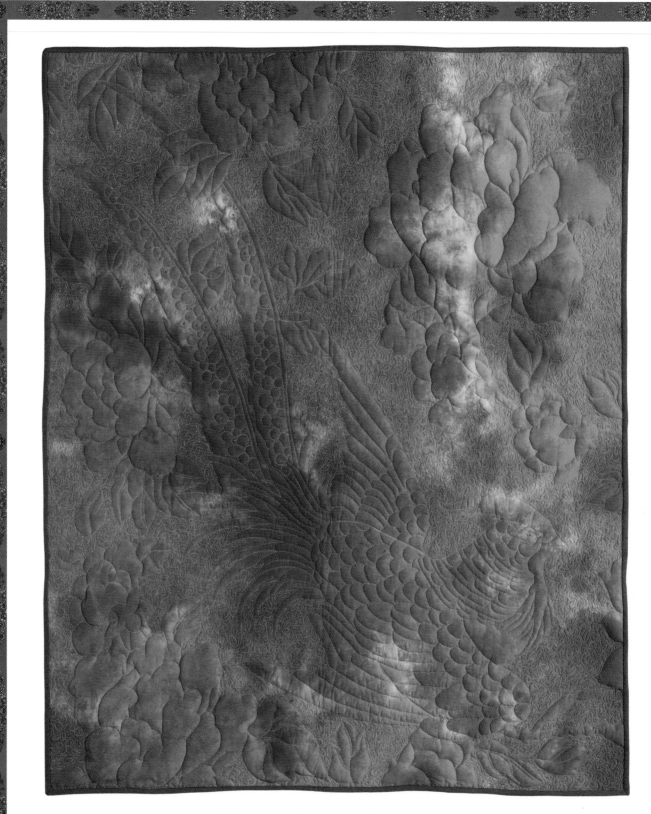

"October Morning" (33" x 41")

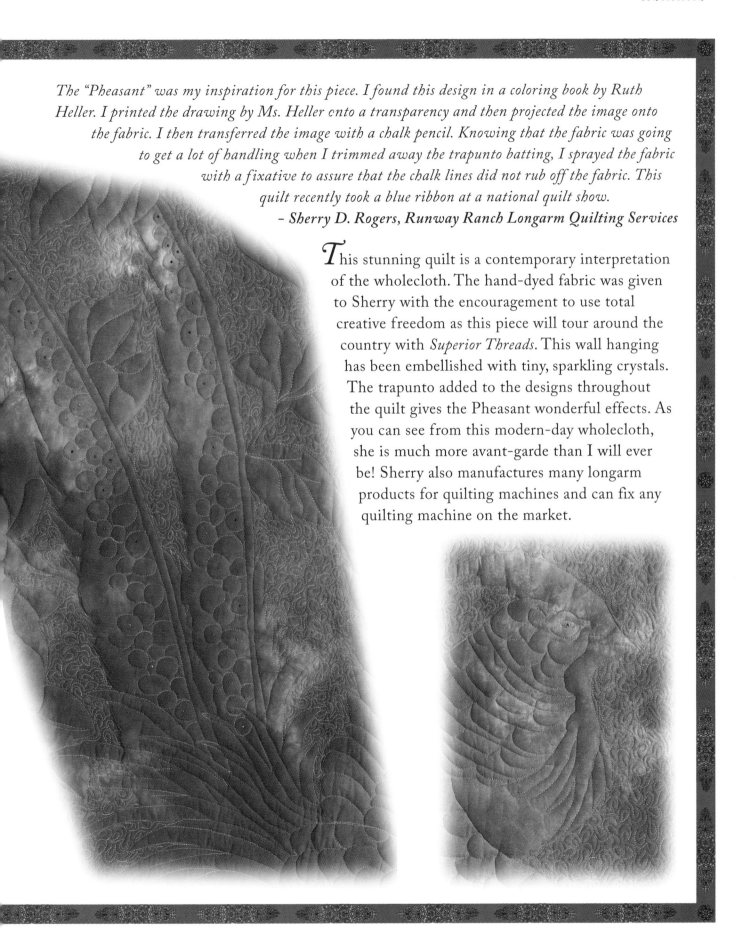

The "Pheasant" was my inspiration for this piece. I found this design in a coloring book by Ruth Heller. I printed the drawing by Ms. Heller onto a transparency and then projected the image onto the fabric. I then transferred the image with a chalk pencil. Knowing that the fabric was going to get a lot of handling when I trimmed away the trapunto batting, I sprayed the fabric with a fixative to assure that the chalk lines did not rub off the fabric. This quilt recently took a blue ribbon at a national quilt show.
– Sherry D. Rogers, Runway Ranch Longarm Quilting Services

This stunning quilt is a contemporary interpretation of the wholecloth. The hand-dyed fabric was given to Sherry with the encouragement to use total creative freedom as this piece will tour around the country with *Superior Threads*. This wall hanging has been embellished with tiny, sparkling crystals. The trapunto added to the designs throughout the quilt gives the Pheasant wonderful effects. As you can see from this modern-day wholecloth, she is much more avant-garde than I will ever be! Sherry also manufactures many longarm products for quilting machines and can fix any quilting machine on the market.

"A Touch of Yellow" (70" x 73")

"A Touch of Yellow" had approximately 3 months of design time. I partially based the outer design on a 1700's wholecloth quilt that I saw a picture of in a book. I used a couple of stencils for some of the center designs but the ones in the leftover spaces are my own designs. I drew everything out with pencil on freezer paper, making changes where needed. Then, I retraced the pencil lines with a black marker to make it easy to see for the final fabric tracing. I taped the freezer paper down to my countertop and then taped my whole piece of muslin over that and used a blue water-soluble pen to trace the designs onto my actual work piece. Then, I placed my trapunto batting under that and

sewed around the outer edges of the designs with water-soluble thread. It took me several evenings to cut away the excess batting. I had pre-washed the cotton batting to help eliminate shrinkage and quilted all the layers together. It took me about 55 hours to do all the quilting on my longarm machine. This quilt has won numerous machine quilting awards in national as well as international shows. - Carol A. Selepec, Create A Stitch

*T*his wholecloth is fashioned after a picture of a 1700's wholecloth quilt from the book, *Piqué de Provence - from the collections of André-Jean Cabanel*. Carol's quilt has done very well in show, winning at national and international levels. It's one of the best examples of whitework wholecloths I have ever seen. In addition to the extraordinary border, the "Touch of Yellow" comes from her hand-dyed trapunto wool batting. The risks are higher when using hand-dyed trapunto batting because there is a chance that bleeding can occur and stain the main quilt top. Carol did have some bleeding when she first soaked her quilt to remove the water-soluble thread and quilt markings, but luckily, there were no permanent stains. Carol is one of the best longarm quilters in the country and I am thrilled she loaned her quilt for the purpose of this book.

"VANILLA CREAM" (40" x 40")

*This is an original wholecloth that I designed in a class with Karen. I used 100% cotton batting as a main batting behind the white trapunto. This created a subtle color change and gives my trapunto more focus. I entered this quilt in our local county fair where it won the first place ribbon! Since finishing this quilt, I've designed another wholecloth quilt that is waiting for my attention. I've also designed a pieced quilt with lots of plain white space for trapunto. I plan to use the same trapunto shading technique (using different shades of white battings to achieve subtle color changes) in my pieced quilt as I did in my wholecloth. - **Kim Stotsenberg, Sew-N-Sew Quilting***

Kim's quilt is interesting because of her chevron background grids and the white trapunto against an off-white, main batting. You can achieve the opposite effect by using an off-white, trapunto batting. After trimming the excess off-white batting away you would use a solid white batting as your main batting for the quilt. This would create slightly darker shading in the motifs, which are trapuntoed, creating dimension and extra definition to the designs. You might even think the designs are appliqué! The scallop border is very pleasing to me and makes this quilt sing a little louder. Overall, this quilt has good impact.

"Homework" (73" x 74")

This quilt was my homework from a wholecloth workshop with Karen. It was my first attempt at wholecloth quilting. I used trapunto in all the stencil work. This quilt, from conception to completion, was an "exhilaratingly humble" experience. I hope it proves to be an inspiration to others who think, "I could never do that!" This quilt is a national, award-winning quilt in the wholecloth category.
-Marsha West, Forgotten Arts

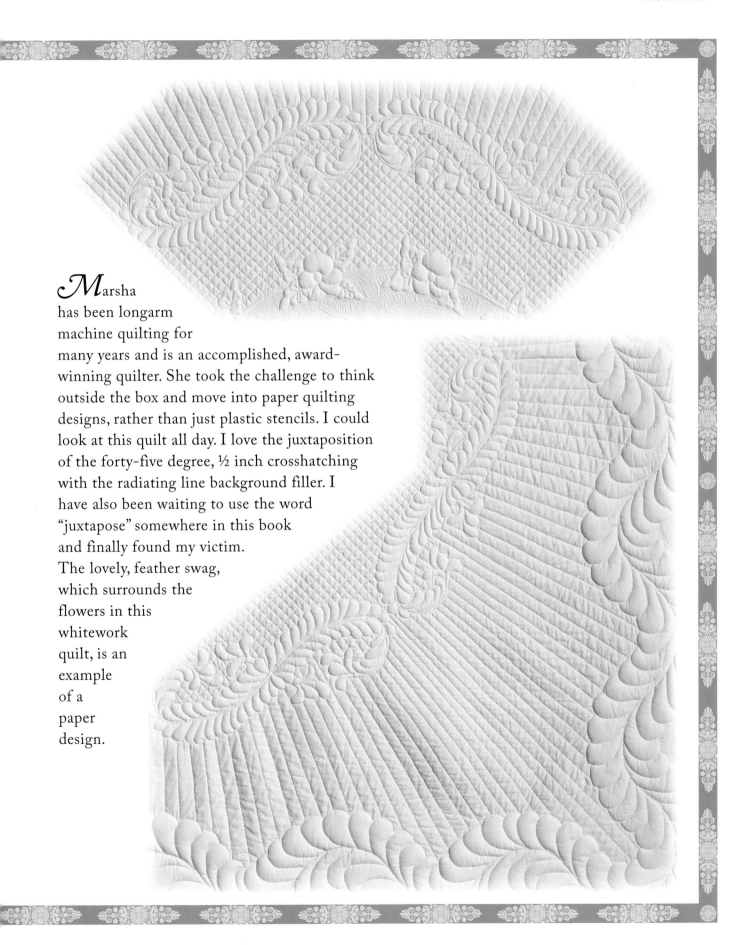

$\mathcal{M}$arsha
has been longarm
machine quilting for
many years and is an accomplished, award-
winning quilter. She took the challenge to think
outside the box and move into paper quilting
designs, rather than just plastic stencils. I could
look at this quilt all day. I love the juxtaposition
of the forty-five degree, ½ inch crosshatching
with the radiating line background filler. I
have also been waiting to use the word
"juxtapose" somewhere in this book
and finally found my victim.
The lovely, feather swag,
which surrounds the
flowers in this
whitework
quilt, is an
example
of a
paper
design.

❧ *Trapunto* ❧

*T*rapunto was first used in clothing. Soldiers wore stuffed clothing for protection from the elements and the enemy, like a medieval bulletproof vest. It may have worked for arrow deflection but could have also caused heat stroke.

The first quilters to use trapunto inserted soft cotton or cording through fine partings in the backing. When the quilts were washed the linen fibers closed over the areas of insertion resulting in the tightly packed, sculptured look. Trapunto was used in both block work and wholecloth work. Quilted counterpanes were either made in the wholecloth style from plain or printed fabrics, or appliqué was used around a large center medallion. Cording and trapunto were popular at the same time as whitework, but were mostly found in communities of Italian immigrants.

Trapunto is used to add texture, shadow and dimension to a quilt. It enhances the motifs and adds extra definition to the desired area. Trapunto is an elegant way to showcase your design. ❧

Traditional Trapunto

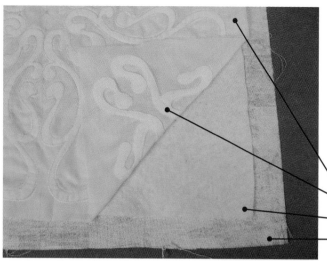

Quilt top
Trapunto batting (trimmed away)
Main batting
Backing

*C*ut-away trapunto is the standard method today. The trapunto batting must be cut away from the back of the quilt top to achieve a beautiful and amazing sculptured effect.

The layers are:

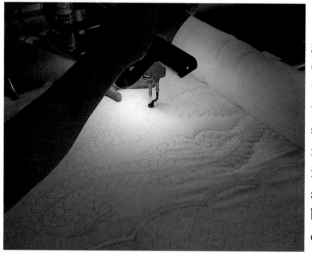

*W*hen you are in the beginning stages of trapunto application, you do not need a quilt backing. First, you must design your quilt top and mark your motifs. (See the Wholecloth chapter for details on designing and marking your quilt top.) After marking the wholecloth, the quilt is ready to start the first stage of trapunto. Load your trapunto batting onto your quilt frame or longarm machine. If you are using a domestic machine, the quilt top must be stretched tight and trapunto batting basted to it. When this is done, you will be looking at a quilt without a backing. This is correct! Add water-soluble thread as your top thread and cotton or poly thread in the bobbin. Pick a bobbin thread color that will not be visible through your finished quilt top or backing. Quilt just the outline of your designs with water-soluble thread. This temporarily holds the trapunto in place as you cut the excess batting away in the next step.

*O*nce you have gone over all the quilting designs that you wish to trapunto in water-soluble thread, remove your quilt from your machine and trim away the batting so that only the quilting design or appliqué has the loft you desire. The trapunto batting will be thick, so be very careful while trimming the batting to avoid snipping the fabric. The scissors I choose to use for trapunto trimming are very sharp, which allows me to get into tight corners and gives me a nice sculptured effect.

$\mathcal{T}$o get a better view when you are trimming your trapunto batting, pull the batting away from the fabric and take tiny, baby snips. The bigger the bite of the scissors; the easier it is to snip the quilt top.

$\mathcal{T}$his is an example of a "snip". It's extremely tiny, but it's there! If you snip the fabric, mark the area with a safety pin so you can find it again when you start the quilting process. This snip is in an area where I will be quilting. When I get to that area I will quilt over the snip several times to cover it up and reinforce the fabric. You can also try a tiny piece of fusible web under the snip, if needed, to keep the edges from fraying. It's a sickening feeling to know you snipped the fabric but the more you practice trapunto trimming, the less this will happen. All good things come with risk.

$\mathcal{T}$his pieced quilt is half way through the trimming stage of trapunto. It's nice to get off my feet once in a while and sit and trim away trapunto batting.

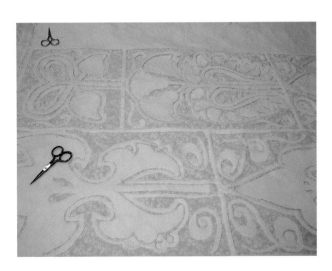

When the trapunto is trimmed, load your machine with the quilt top, a new layer of batting, and the quilt backing material. Quilt the layers as usual, carefully quilting with regular thread on top of the water-soluble thread. Add details to the trapunto designs and the other designs, outlines, and background patterns that will appear on your quilt top.

Once you have finished quilting the quilt, it is the "Moment of Truth." It's time to get rid of all of the blue marking pen and the water-soluble thread. This is a very exciting time as you are very close to your finished project. However, the removal of the water-soluble products can cause some concern because disaster seems to rear its ugly head during this phase. When soaking any quilt in water, you may end up with undesired results such as bleeding, shrinking, or spotting. Making sure your quilt top only has fabrics that have been pre-washed is critical. I do not recommend trapunto on any quilt top which has not been pre-washed as bleeding often occurs with colored fabric. Fill the tub or a large washing machine with warm water and completely immerse your quilt. This will dissolve the water-soluble thread and the blue marks all at once.

"For the Love of Feathers" (45"x 45")

This is my first attempt at a wholecloth quilt. I started it in a workshop with Karen McTavish. I used stencils and achieved extremely tiny micro-stippling. This quilt won a national, blue-ribbon award in a wholecloth challenge in September 2002. It was an incredible learning experience!
– Mary A. Bojan, Flying Needle Custom Machine Quilting

This is a national award-winning quilt with great visual appeal. The radiating lines used as background filler in her borders are very effective. This design pulls your attention to the fancy border instead of drawing your eyes to the centerpiece. Bringing the eye to the middle of the quilt should be your goal, but this composition has a nice appeal. The traditional, classic, feather centerpiece, coupled with the blindingly-tiny, micro-stippling Mary was able to achieve, became the perfect choice for an uncomplicated medallion. Her combination of quilting and use of stencils created a powerful impact. This may have been what sparked the judges' interests and gave her the blue ribbon nod of approval.

"A Study in White" (35" x 35")

This was my first attempt at an original wholecloth quilt. I took the wholecloth workshop with Sherry Rogers, and later with Karen McTavish, to learn the entire process. I love color and scrap quilts - for me, the more fabrics the better! This plain, wholecloth quilt pushed me out of my comfort zone. I was determined to finish it and am thrilled at the result. I have since taken Karen's class again, and tackled another color-batting/shadow-trapunto wholecloth as well! – **Marcia J. Bowen**

Marcia's award-winning talent is evident from the visual impact her quilt makes. When I first pointed out that her wholecloth could handle a ¼ inch crosshatching background grid, she looked at me like I was out of my mind. But she did it! This impressive background filler, which is hardly forgiving, makes the perfect, delicate statement for a very lady-like wholecloth. The frames separate the background grids allowing one background filler to stop and another to be introduced. A note of caution: judging points are not added to your quilt based on the complexity or difficulty of the quilting technique (such as ¼ inch crosshatching). If you are going to attempt something challenging, you must execute it well as Marcia did here.

"Arctic Art" (36" x 36")

*This original design is the product of the wholecloth workshop I attended with Karen McTavish.
I wanted to make a small project since this was my first attempt at designing a wholecloth from
scratch and using machine trapunto. The top started out at 40" x 40" and after quilting, washing and
blocking the quilt, it finished up at 36" x 36". This was such a fun challenge; I am definitely hooked
and look forward to using what I learned from this wholecloth project as well as trying new and
different techniques on future projects. - Sherri Dolly, Scrap Basket Quilting*

This quilt is the classic white on white. It is a perfect example of following the rules of wholecloth tradition. This quilt may be small, but it is so well balanced, with a clean, crisp feel that it knocks my socks off. The scallop border is perfectly placed without any sign of problems with its connection. The background grids are ever changing; notice the different angles and sizes of crosshatching used throughout this quilt. Sherri gave her center motif the appearance of cording by adding trapunto to her frames and leaf work. The scallop border looks fabulous and it is rich with that traditional, classic look.

"PANSY GARDEN" (50" x 50")

As a child, my favorite part of my grandmother's garden was the pansies. This quilt, begun in a class with Karen, allowed me to combine my lifelong love of pansies with some of my favorite quilting elements: feathers, background cross-hatching and stippling. This wholecloth project has been a very rewarding experience for me. Karen has demonstrated to all her students that we can do far more than we think we can! **- Monty Sue Haubold, Monty's Flying Needle**

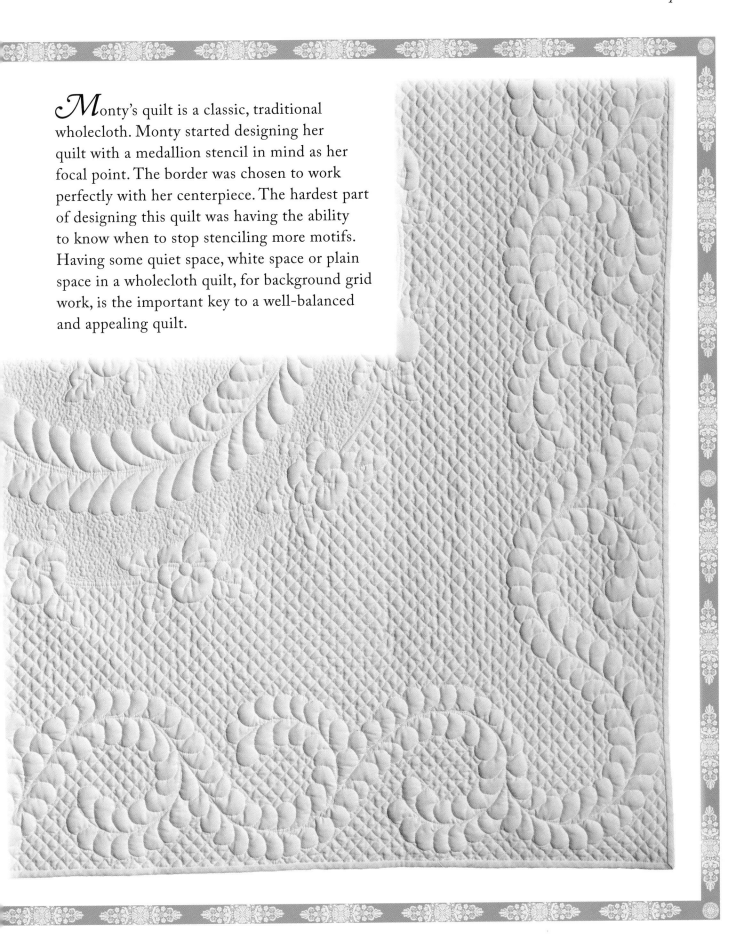

$\mathcal{M}$onty's quilt is a classic, traditional wholecloth. Monty started designing her quilt with a medallion stencil in mind as her focal point. The border was chosen to work perfectly with her centerpiece. The hardest part of designing this quilt was having the ability to know when to stop stenciling more motifs. Having some quiet space, white space or plain space in a wholecloth quilt, for background grid work, is the important key to a well-balanced and appealing quilt.

"Rose Garden" (60" x 65")

After being inspired by Karen's wholecloth quilts, I created "Rose Garden" in her workshop. This original wholecloth incorporates trapunto and a very subtle variegated thread on unbleached muslin. I have been a longarm machine quilter since 2002 but have been quilting for years and was excited to complete my first wholecloth. This wholecloth is a national award-winning quilt.

- Jacqueline M. Kamlet, Painting with Stitches

This is a great example of the contrast you can get in a wholecloth when your trapunto batting is white and your main batting is off-white. The result of this technique is that the trapunto looks like white appliqué, which is an excellent effect. No short cuts (such as faux trapunto) were taken with this quilt. Jacqueline's efforts to cut away the trapunto in the border must have taken her at least 20 hours. Trimming trapunto batting away from tight spots, such as the stems, leaves and flowers, paid off in the end. A floral border with matching centerpiece seems to be pleasing to the judges. Adding some contemporary background fillers, such as "McTavishing" pushes the traditional wholecloth envelope but Jacqueline's choice seemed more exciting than plain stippling. Stippling is starting to become boring to judges; they are looking for alternative background fillers. This labor-intensive quilt recently received a ribbon in a national quilt show.

"Moosely Feathered Friends" (68" x 68")

"Moosely Feathered Friends" is an original wholecloth quilt I designed in a class taught by Karen McTavish and Sherry Rogers. My business, "MooseQuilteers," hosted the "Queens of Wholecloth." I wanted a very traditional wholecloth quilt so I chose feather stencils to create a wonderful border and feather and flowers for the center. I named the quilt as a reminder of the teachers I had and the good friends I made during class. I still treasure the memories when I look at my wholecloth. I had to close my business and move to Denver, due to family emergency in March, 2002, but continue to quilt as much as I can. - Aurora Lowell, MooseQuilteers

*A*urora's traditional wholecloth is so gentle and soft. It amazes me that the material in Aurora's hands was fabric one minute and her first wholecloth masterpiece the next minute! This wholecloth quilt was juried and selected as a contestant in a major quilt show in 2002 and was the only original wholecloth in the entire show. This is a first-class example of a wholecloth quilt that shows plenty of "breathing room" or "white space." It can be very difficult to know when to stop adding more stencil designs to the wholecloth and walk away.

"Baskets in Paradise" (72" x 74")

Making this original wholecloth quilt was a great way to stretch my creativity. I was able to take a few of my favorite things - feathers, flowers and baskets - and combine them into a fabulous design! This is my first wholecloth and it recently won an "Honorable Mention" award at a national quilt show. - Becky Manske, Becky's Custom Quilting

*T*his is a wholecloth with a chunky, powerful border. I like that. Becky's quilt has two wonderful assets: appliqué-like trapunto (caused by off-white, main cotton batting) and originality. Her borders are balanced and well placed. The large size of Becky's quilt allowed her to use a big, fat, border stencil. She complemented the outsized border by adding a large central focal point. Becky's quilt is currently "in show" all over the country and will be for the next two years. When I last spoke to Becky she was starting her second wholecloth.

"GRANDMOTHER" (60" x 60")

My love for the traditional, wholecloth quilt has existed as far back as I can remember. I am an enrolled member of the Cow Creek Band of the Umpqua Tribe of Indians in Oregon. The quilt was named "Grandmother" to show honor and respect to our tribal elders. This original wholecloth embodies my respect for the traditional. The use of longarm machine quilting has challenged me to maintain the integrity of past generations while creatively combining vision with contemporary techniques. This quilt has been shown regionally and was awarded multiple blue ribbons, along with "Judges Choice" in textiles. - **Carole Denny-Oelrich, Eagle's Nest Quilting Studio**

*C*arole's quilt is a remarkable example of the different statement each wholecloth quilt makes. Her quilt is like no other, and her interpretations of traditions are based on her heritage, not the wholecloth history. This makes her quilt even more special. Her stencil designs work well together because they are generally the same size and shape. This stunning quilt shows the beautiful trapunto effects of using off-white, fabric with bright white, poly trapunto batting. Her center motif was modified and repeated on-point, which crafts a unique medallion.

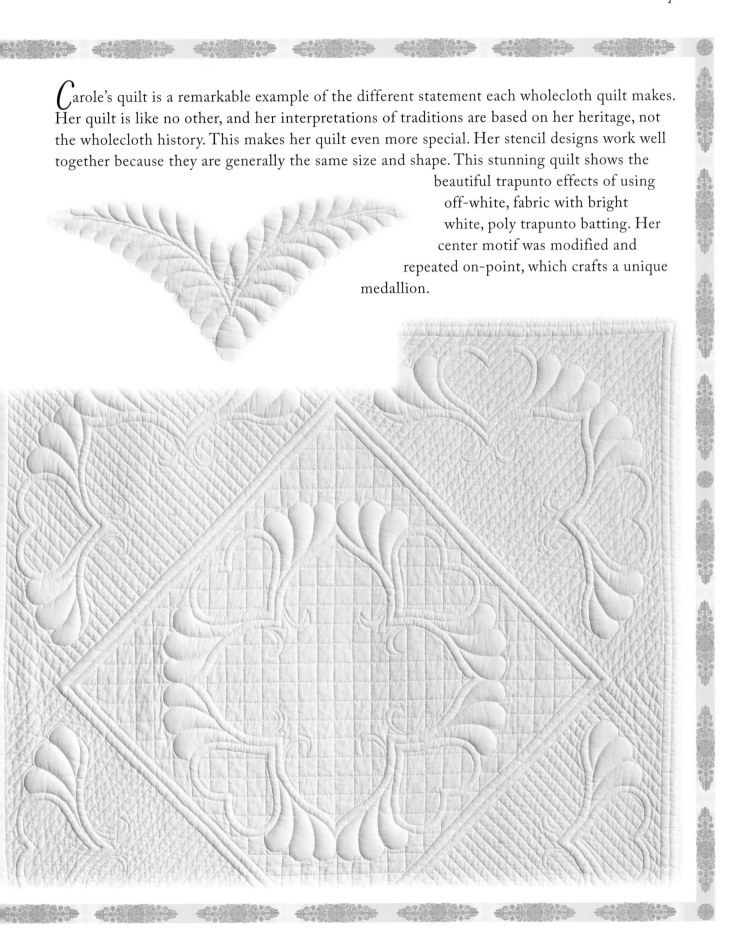

"MY MASTERPIECE" (40 ½" x 54 ½")

This is my first wholecloth quilt which I designed in Karen's class in 2002. The quilting was a personal challenge and I am very proud of it. I am pleased and amazed that I finished it!
- Betty Peine, Sweet Dreams Machine Quilting

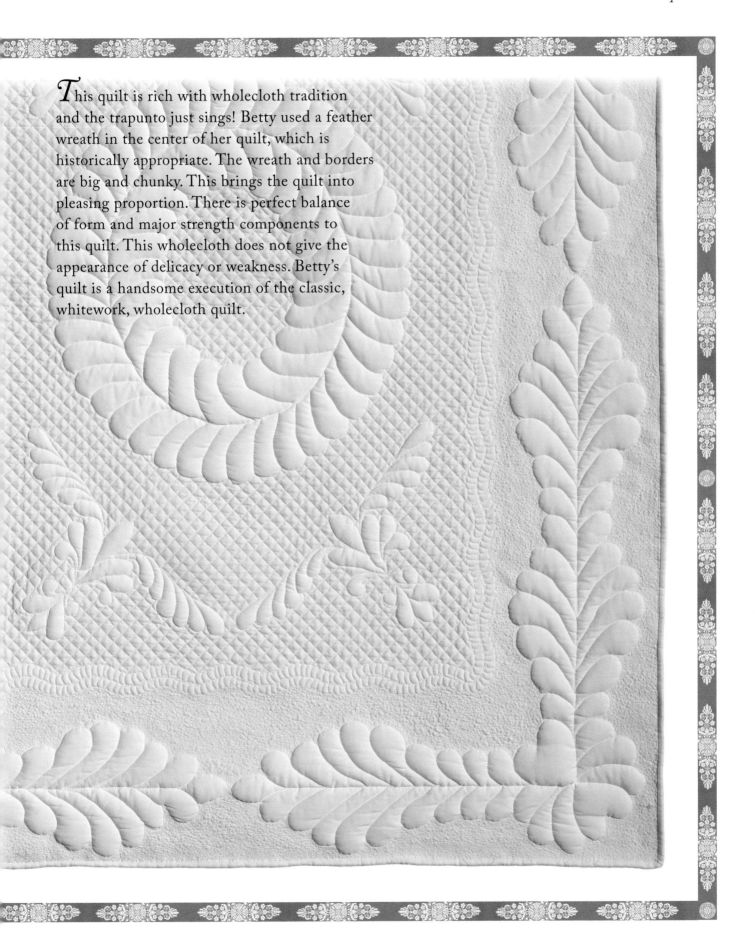

This quilt is rich with wholecloth tradition and the trapunto just sings! Betty used a feather wreath in the center of her quilt, which is historically appropriate. The wreath and borders are big and chunky. This brings the quilt into pleasing proportion. There is perfect balance of form and major strength components to this quilt. This wholecloth does not give the appearance of delicacy or weakness. Betty's quilt is a handsome execution of the classic, whitework, wholecloth quilt.

"Floral Bouquet" (54" x 73")

"Floral Bouquet" is my first wholecloth trapunto project. A rose quilting stencil inspired my original design. Begun at a workshop with Karen McTavish, I found the process was certainly time-consuming but very gratifying and extremely rewarding. It was quilted on my hand-guided, longarm quilting machine. The entire project was completed in six weeks, motivated by a deadline for a quilt show. As this was the first time I had entered any judged show, I was astounded that it took a red ribbon at the national level. The quilt has also taken ribbons at a state quilt show, a regional quilt show, and has been juried into several other national shows.
– Janice E. Petre, Janice Petre's House of Quilting

Janice's quilt has an unusually strong design which compliments her stencil and trapunto work. The shape of her fabric is oblong, which is very traditional. She incorporated roses into her center and two borders, reminding me of a bridal quilt. This whitework piece becomes more intricate with the addition of ¼ inch, parallel, chevron, background quilting (straight line quilting) located in the on-point sections of the frame. The frame itself looks to be corded, but is actually trapunto, carefully trimmed to give the appearance of cord work. This is a national award-winning quilt.

"Heirloom Roses" (57" x 57")

This national award-winning, original wholecloth evolved from a workshop with Karen McTavish. I used cotton muslin on the front and back of this quilt. The quilting designs are original as well as motifs pulled from different stencils. This quilt has won both a "Viewer's Choice" award and a "Faculty Choice" ribbon. I enjoy the wholecloth experience – each project is an exercise in creativity and spawns new ideas for future quilts. - **Sandra D. Reed, Creative Machine Quilting**

Sandra's quilt has fabulous visual impact. She was able to modify her feather borders using one half of one side of one stencil. This stencil was flipped back and forth to create a mirror image for her borders. A very crisp, formal effect is achieved by the regularity of her feather frame that surrounds her centerpiece. She added a high loft trapunto batting to give the quilting designs extra enhancement. A whitework quilt goes farther in quilt shows by showing excellent construction: good thread tension, consistent stitching and good starts and stops.

"WHAT WAS I THINKING!?" (40" x 40")

In April of 2002, I took a wholecloth class with Karen McTavish. I have always loved wholecloth quilts. When I took the class I did not even have a longarm machine; I had a very basic, shortarm quilting machine. Soon after taking the class I found out that we would be moving to New Jersey. I sold my shortarm machine and bought a longarm quilting machine. It was delivered to my new home in August 2002. I practiced for about a month and decided I would quilt my wholecloth. What was I thinking!? This was the first quilt I quilted on my longarm. It turned out fairly well for a first quilt and I am pleased with the end result. - Cathy Rogers, Cherry Hill Quilter

*I*t's just not fair that Cathy's first machine quilted wholecloth turned into a masterpiece. My first quilt certainly did not look like this. Cathy's wholecloth design is an excellent example of the 18th century needlework called "whitework." While in the 18th century it could take hundreds of hours to hand quilt; Cathy only took 10 hours on her longarm. The quilt's beauty holds the integrity of fine quality craftsmanship seen in quilts from one hundred years ago. There is a perfect balance to this quilt and the overall impact is eye catching. Cathy took the leap by designing small buttons in her frame around the center motif. This takes precision and patience. For a first time wholecloth quilt – it had to be intimidating.

"STEMS & STITCHES, ESTABLISHED 2001" (53" x 55")

This original quilt is my first attempt at wholecloth trapunto quilting. It was designed in Karen's class in October 2002 and finished in December of that same year. This quilt is 100% cotton muslin, front and back. My machine quilting business name, "Stems & Stitches," is quilted above the center medallion along with the date my business was established (2001). I am so proud to have completed this quilt. - **Kathy J. Slater, Stems & Stitches**

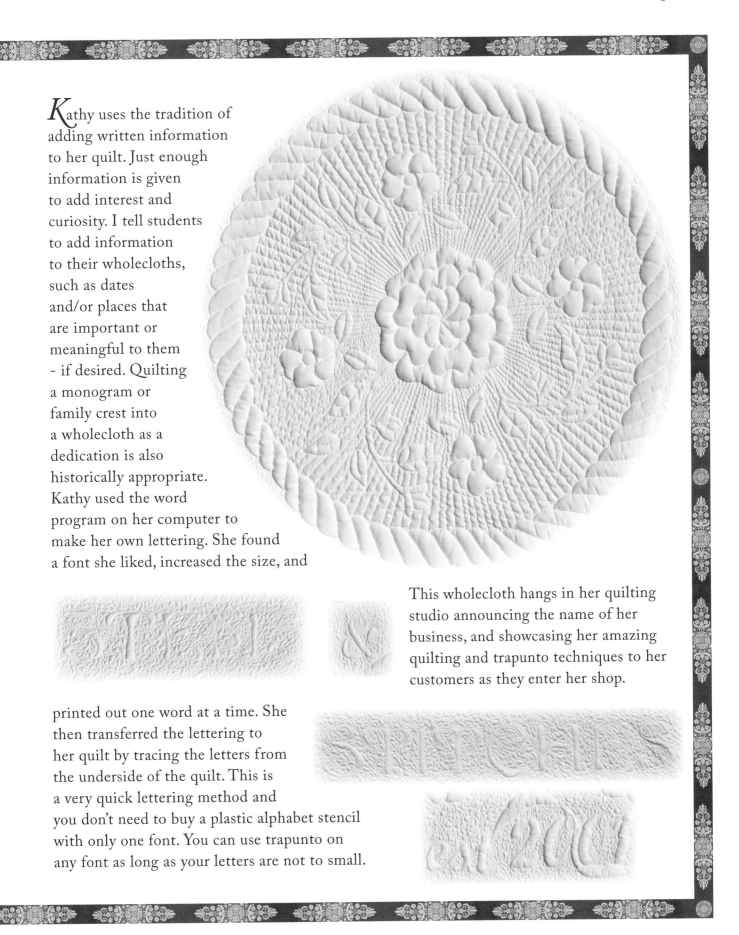

Kathy uses the tradition of adding written information to her quilt. Just enough information is given to add interest and curiosity. I tell students to add information to their wholecloths, such as dates and/or places that are important or meaningful to them - if desired. Quilting a monogram or family crest into a wholecloth as a dedication is also historically appropriate. Kathy used the word program on her computer to make her own lettering. She found a font she liked, increased the size, and

This wholecloth hangs in her quilting studio announcing the name of her business, and showcasing her amazing quilting and trapunto techniques to her customers as they enter her shop.

printed out one word at a time. She then transferred the lettering to her quilt by tracing the letters from the underside of the quilt. This is a very quick lettering method and you don't need to buy a plastic alphabet stencil with only one font. You can use trapunto on any font as long as your letters are not to small.

"HEAVENLY FEATHERS" (53" x 55")

This is the very first wholecloth quilt that I designed and quilted. The feather design in the border is one of my favorites, so it was a natural choice. I marked every line of the ¼ inch crosshatching directly onto the quilt top to make sure they were perfectly straight and at a forty-five degree angle. I also used micro-stippling as a heavy, background filler. I enjoyed the process of creating and quilting this quilt immensely and I am very pleased with the results. - Barbara R. Tibus, Quilts to Treasure

$\mathcal{B}$arbara's border background quilting is a very respectable and brave ¼ inch, straight-line chevron, which she marked with a plastic ruler, one line at a time. This grid work was carried into the middle of the quilt with ¼ inch crosshatching. To top this off, as if we weren't already impressed, she added micro-stippling as a heavy filler which makes her feathers jump out of her quilt. The on-point, feather design in the center of the wholecloth acts as a frame surrounding a smaller design. This design has rarely been used to create part of a medallion. Barbara auditioned the stencil and repeated the design four times in order to surround the small motif in the middle of the quilt. I would have never thought of this. The creativity of her design and resulting one-of-a-kind wholecloth came from a beautiful mind.

Color Trapunto

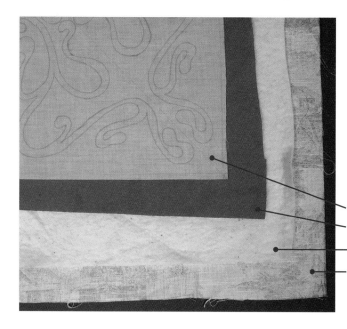

*T*his is a new style of trapunto. Instead of white poly batting - dyed batting, fleece print, or a large piece of felt is used. These fabrics are used as the trapunto batting and trimmed away just like regular trapunto work.

The layers are:

Quilt top (translucent or semi-translucent)
Bright neon felt or dyed trapunto batting
Main batting
Backing

*T*o achieve color trapunto you will need a wide piece of bright colored acrylic felt. Your quilt top fabric must be somewhat sheer, such as batiste, so the color trapunto will be seen. Acrylic felt and batiste can be found in most craft and fabric stores. I like to use the brightest acrylic felt available as the results will be more vivid.

*O*nce the wholecloth has been entirely marked load it and the color backing, such as acrylic felt, on to your machine. This is the first stage of color trapunto.

Now pin the wholecloth top directly to the acrylic felt and load your quilting machine with water-soluble thread. Your bobbin thread is not water-soluble so pick a color that won't show inside the finished quilt. In this case, white was used.

Now, outline the areas where you want color trapunto using water-soluble thread. Be very careful to stay on the marked blue line.

Because water-soluble thread is temporarily holding my color batting in place, I can "drag" my thread to the next quilting area where trapunto will be added. Securing stitches is not an issue at this stage, but good tension is important. To avoid breakage, you may have to loosen your tension to use this lightweight thread.

$\mathcal{L}$ongarm quilting machines are hand guided and are very free-motion. You can use a ruler to gain more control as you carefully outline the areas you want trapunto.

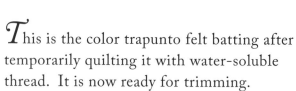

$\mathcal{T}$his is the color trapunto felt batting after temporarily quilting it with water-soluble thread. It is now ready for trimming.

$\mathcal{A}$ccurate trimming is very important. Any untrimmed color batting will show through as "seepage" or "shadowing". It will be as clear as day when the final quilting is done. Quilt show judges are more concerned that the color trapunto technique is done well and don't give points for design difficulty. Guess how I know this.

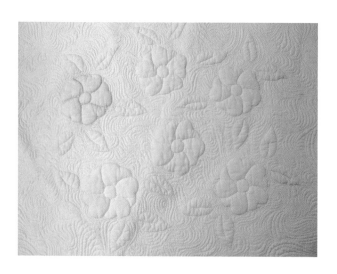

$\mathcal{T}$o see which color batting will bleed in warm water, I like to do a test run first. You can see 6 flowers; each flower has a different color and a different fiber: wool, wool-blend, acrylic felt, wool felt, etc. After dunking the test piece in warm water, I could judge which color batting worked well and which did not by the amount of bleeding. The two flowers that did not bleed used acrylic felt, which can be found in most retail fabric stores. Remember - the darker the color you choose, the muddier the color will appear.

The Making of ~ "Because It's Just Harder to Appliqué"

This shows the process of creating my whitework wholecloth, *Because It's Just Harder to Appliqué*. When the entire quilt was completely marked, I moved into the trapunto phase. I added trapunto to the borders first by using regular poly trapunto batting. Once I trimmed the fat poly batting away, I started the color trapunto process.

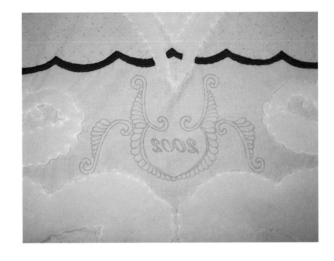

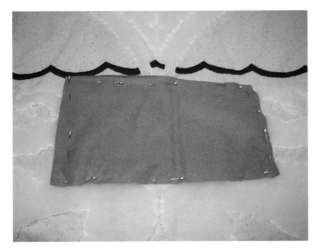

I placed a piece of bright pink acrylic felt on the underside of the area where I wanted color. I pinned the felt in place making sure to keep the pins away from where my needle will strike.

After pinning the acrylic felt in place I quilted an outline of my design with water-soluble thread and white bobbin thread. Now I can see where to trim away the extra batting.

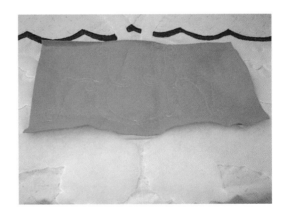

Here is my design after trimming away the excess batting. I decided to use bright red acrylic felt for my lettering of the year 2002. I can add as many colors as I want to the quilt as long as I am willing to continue to trim away the excess batting.

*H*ere is an excellent example of a corner motif before it is trimmed. You can clearly see the colored felt beneath the translucent top. I need to outline the motif with water-soluble thread and then take the quilt off the frame for trimming.

*N*otice how sculptured the motif looks on this design and how clean the snips appear. This is achieved by carefully trimming with sharp, pointy scissors.

*T*his is an example of what the underside of your quilt could look like after several colors of felt batting are added and the excess trimmed away from the designs. Having table space and plenty of trashcans in your studio help keep this process nice and neat.

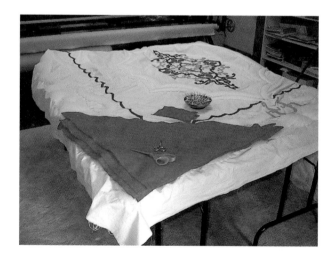

At this stage, I am quilting the top, batting, and backing together using machine quilting thread. I have quilted the outline of the color trapunto first. Being accurate is extremely important at this stage. If you do not follow the marked blue lines exactly as you quilt, it will appear as if the motif did not receive the proper amount of color (too much or not enough) and will be very noticeable.

This quilt's backing is white cotton sateen, which is now available in very wide fabrics. As you can see, none of the color trapunto shows through. This dense and opaque fabric works great for the backing but the fabric you pick for the quilt top should be translucent or semi-translucent when using the color batting technique.

My trapunto has been quilted but the plain space is slightly wavy. When the background fillers have been quilted the quilt will lay flat.

When you are finished quilting your quilt it is time to soak out the blue marking pen and the water-soluble thread in warm water. After the quilt markings have disappeared, double check the water-soluble thread to make sure it has completely dissolved. If the quilt dries without the water-soluble thread dissolving first, it may turn into a hard brittle mess. Re-soaking the quilt in hot water will dissolve any water-soluble thread that did not dissolve the first time.

"Because It's Just Harder to Appliqué" (89"x 94")

𝒯his original, wholecloth quilt is the result of learning from mistakes I have made on prior wholecloth quilts. This wholecloth combines "color trapunto" with traditional trapunto. The color comes from bright red acrylic felt used under the fabric as trapunto batting, which creates a shadow of pink. I used several different red and pink felts to achieve the different hues in the trapunto. I developed this technique after trying many different types of fibers; this method seemed to be the most successful. The backing is cotton sateen. I was inspired by the quilting style of Beverly Mannisto Williams. This is the most rewarding wholecloth I have ever designed and quilted because disaster was avoided. This quilt has taken several local and national awards including Best of Show and Best Longarm Machine Quilting. - *Karen McTavish*

"The Phat Batt" (60" x 60")

$\mathcal{T}$his was a fun experiment gone terribly wrong. This was my first attempt at using a 20 ounce trapunto batting. This batting is very dense and thick, possibly the thickest that should ever be used in trapunto. It was so thick I had to raise my hopping foot to quilt over the feathers. I loved this quilt for several reasons before its demise. The off-white, main batting of the quilt is 100% cotton. It created noticeable contrast between the white trapunto and the background

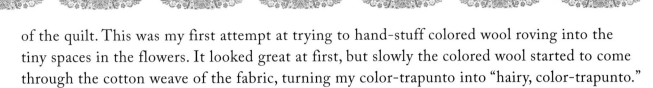

of the quilt. This was my first attempt at trying to hand-stuff colored wool roving into the tiny spaces in the flowers. It looked great at first, but slowly the colored wool started to come through the cotton weave of the fabric, turning my color-trapunto into "hairy, color-trapunto." At the time of this photo, the quilt was still on its best behavior. But now, I have to shave the colored wool fibers that can be seen coming through the fabric. I have since come up with a much better way to achieve color-trapunto without any bleeding, shrinking or shaving. (See "Because it's Just Harder to Appliqué" - my latest color trapunto quilt.) – *Karen McTavish*

"Thanks to Rose Kretsinger" (48" x 48")

I love any quilting design created by Rose Kretsinger, especially the *Rose Kretsinger Scroll.* This is another trapunto-gone-wrong experiment. I used 100% wool roving, dyed red, as an alternative to plain white poly trapunto. After designing and marking the quilt, I hand-stuffed the roving into areas where I wanted extra color. The disaster came after I had finished the entire quilt and was ready to remove the water-soluble products. I dunked the quilt in the

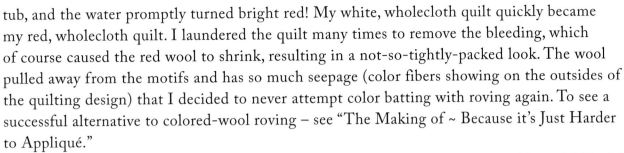

tub, and the water promptly turned bright red! My white, wholecloth quilt quickly became my red, wholecloth quilt. I laundered the quilt many times to remove the bleeding, which of course caused the red wool to shrink, resulting in a not-so-tightly-packed look. The wool pulled away from the motifs and has so much seepage (color fibers showing on the outsides of the quilting design) that I decided to never attempt color batting with roving again. To see a successful alternative to colored-wool roving – see "The Making of ~ Because it's Just Harder to Appliqué."

– *Karen McTavish*

"A Serpentine Tale" (36" x 36")

This original, wholecloth wall hanging was machine quilted as a class project after attending a private workshop in Karen's studio. I chose this pattern as it reminds me of the beautiful, sinuous vines and leaves I saw while driving to Karen's studio in Northern Minnesota. I used bright-red, acrylic felt as the colored batting, which gives my quilt a subtle suggestion of pink. The quilt top is 100% cotton batiste. This was also my first attempt at micro-stippling. I am very pleased with the finished project! - Beverly Sievers, Dancing Threads Heirloom Machine Quilting

*B*everly's quilt was a commitment and challenge. She chose a border and its matching centerpiece as her focus. She later added the leaf design as her center frame. She also used colored batting instead of a poly batting. If you are not familiar with color batting, this quilt could make you wonder how it is done! Beverly said it took hours to trim the red, trapunto batting from the quilt top. It is important to remember that when you are using white, sheer, batiste fabric, you will be able to see every single

detail - including the color batting and how it was trimmed. In judged competition, you may hear to watch for "seeping" or "cloudy around the edges." It is so important in this technique to cut and trim the color portion of the batting cleanly, without snipping the quilt top in the cutting process (which is very easy to do on this fabric). Cut as carefully as possible when using any sheer fabric.

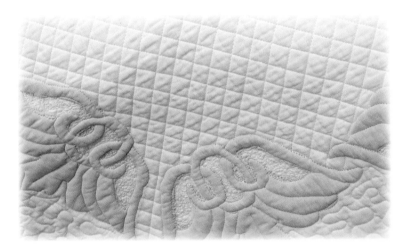

Shadow Trapunto

*T*his technique uses one piece of fabric for the quilted top but gives the illusion of dyed batting and appliqué. The illusion is achieved using a translucent or semi-translucent fabric top. Make your design using the techniques taught in wholecloth design and traditional trapunto. Before final quilting, slip in a neon bright piece of fabric under the quilt top and on top of the batting to give a shadow of color through the sheer fabric. You may have also heard this called Positive/Negative Trapunto.

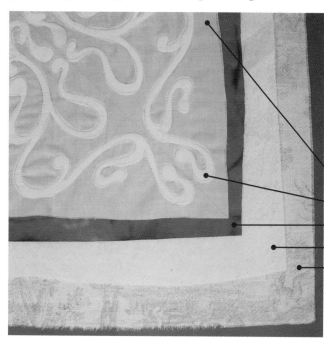

The layers are:

Quilt top (translucent or semi-translucent)
Trapunto batting (white - trimmed away)
Bright neon fabric (under the trapunto batting)
Main batting
Backing

Trapunto Styles Overview

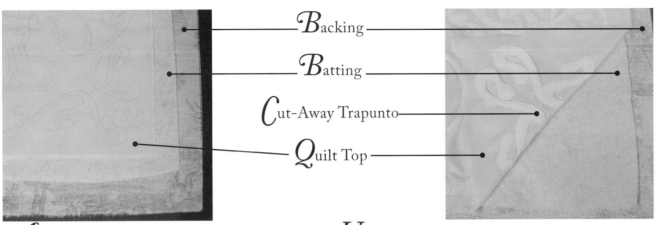

*B*acking

*B*atting

*C*ut-Away Trapunto

*Q*uilt Top

*A*ll trapunto quilts start with a backing, batting and marked quilt top.

*U*se a white poly batting for traditional cut-away trapunto.

*B*acking

*B*atting

*C*olor Felt Cut-Away Trapunto

*Q*uilt Top

*C*olor trapunto uses colored acrylic felt for trapunto instead of a white poly batting.

*T*he colored acrylic felt cut-away trapunto stands out after quilting a background filler.

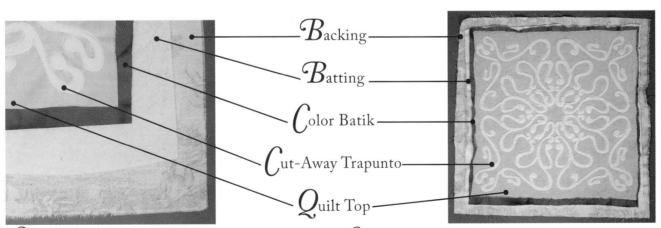

*B*acking

*B*atting

*C*olor Batik

*C*ut-Away Trapunto

*Q*uilt Top

*S*hadow trapunto adds a bright colored fabric between the quilt top and the main batting.

*S*hadow trapunto creates the illusion of color batting with an appliqué top.

"WEDGWOOD BLUE" (42" x 42")

This wall hanging uses a sheer, white, batiste fabric as the wholecloth top. Using the technique called "Shadow Trapunto" a neon blue piece of fabric is placed between the layers of the quilt, producing the light blue color. The result of shadow trapunto is a very soft looking quilt, with a two-tone appearance. This wall hanging is very appealing to me and was a small enough project to be enjoyable from start to finish. – Melanie Austin, Huckleberry Stitches Custom Machine Quilting

This shadow trapunto wall hanging is the result of Melanie's first attempt working with white, batiste fabric. The neon-blue batik she chose created a stunning "after color" which comes through as a pale, baby blue. The misconception that the color comes from dyed batting or that the white trapunto is actually white fabric which has been appliquéd directly onto the blue fabric has the desired effect - to fool the eye! For those who do not want to commit to an appliqué project, or who want to play with different forms of trapunto, shadow trapunto is a great alternative.

"Springtime in Clover Valley" (84" x 84")

Clover Valley, on the north shore of Lake Superior, is in the township where my family resides. The "square in a square" inspiration came from a mother/daughter trip to the International Quilt show in Houston. The idea came together on the flight home to Minnesota. My mother loves color, unlike her daughter who prefers white. I wanted to quilt a wholecloth using shadow trapunto, but had construction problems from the start. The options for a large, shadow-trapunto, wholecloth quilt were very limited because there was not large width fabrics available in batiste. My mother had to piece the simple "square in a square" using 60 inch wide Swiss batiste, which was special-ordered from www.sewbaby.com. This quilt uses shadow trapunto to create the different colors; it does not have dyed batting. The batiste quilt top was originally all white but when neon fabrics are inserted between the quilting layers, the color starts to appear. When the final quilting is completed, the color really comes to

the forefront. My mother pieced the entire quilt, using miniature piecing in the sashing, which strategically hid the white seams of the batiste and the raw edges of the neon fabrics. My mother won her first blue ribbon in a national competition with this quilt.

- Jan and Karen McTavish

"Red Shadow Trapunto" (30" x 30")

$\mathcal{T}$his was my first attempt at shadow trapunto. This wall hanging was made with white batiste and an 80/20 trapunto batting. I had fun auditioning different fabrics under the batiste to see what color would result. I used a red batik fabric, washed first to avoid bleeding. I added my last name, city, state, and date. I needed one more informational word so I added my first

name because I couldn't think of anything else to include! The letters came from my computer "word" program. I simply printed the word in a font that I liked and traced the words directly on to the fabric. The letters were tiny, which required very precise trimming so the words could be easily readable. – *Karen McTavish*

"BELLA ROSA" (56" x 56")

*I never imagined that a shadow trapunto quilt would be so effective in the quilting world. This quilt has won many national awards, which makes it easier for me to tell you how difficult this project was for me! The muslin I picked for my wholecloth was nearly opaque; it seemed like no fabric could create enough contrast after being placed behind the muslin to see any color change. Who would have guessed that it took a fluorescent-yellow fabric to create the subtle, cream and white effect I had initially desired? Bella! - **Michelle L. Miller, The Quilter's Cabin***

*I*t seems that no matter where I travel in the country, when I get to the wholecloth section of a quilt show, I see Michelle's quilt with a big, blue ribbon on it. Michelle's cream colored quilt looks very traditional - floral, with a touch of feathers - but has just enough color to raise some eyebrows. This unique wholecloth seems to intrigue the quilt judges. Michelle did two shadow trapunto pieces when she took a private workshop with me. Both were beautiful! The "Quilters Dream Poly" trapunto batting she used in the featured quilt, was the perfect loft. The quilt hangs very straight and has good balance and design. Thread tension, construction of the quilt and stitch consistency all passed their tests, which is why this quilt is an award-winner.

"PRETTY IN PINK" (54" x 56")

I hosted Karen McTavish at my shop in July 2003. I decided to sit in on her "Wholecloth Trapunto Extravaganza" workshop. I had never attempted trapunto and was eager to learn a new technique. This is by far the best class I have ever taken. It gave me the opportunity to learn "heirloom" traditional quilting. I was amazed at the success of my first project and am honored Karen has included it in this book. I was able to finish the layout, design work, shadow trapunto and quilting within 55 hours – start to finish! - Sue Schmieden, The Quilting Connection

Sue's quilt is amazing. She made one mistake that turned into something I have to share in this book. When I was teaching my color batting technique, Sue was in and out of the classroom, dealing with her customers, the phones and all the things she needed to take care of as the hostess of the

trapunto batting away from her quilt top and just needed some neon fabric to place between the quilt layers – since she wanted shadow trapunto only. Instead of using a bright fabric to create the color she wanted, she used neon pink acrylic felt. The result of her using a thick felt, instead of a

workshop. She heard that she needed "colored acrylic felt" for her wholecloth to achieve color - true, but not quite the whole story. The felt really applies to the colored batting technique I was teaching, not shadow trapunto technique. Sue had already trimmed her white, poly

piece of thin fabric, is a plush, full-bodied wholecloth. Her color is paler and softer than the standard shadow trapunto. Her quilt could be called, "My Colored Shadow Trapunto Using Acrylic Felt Wholecloth Method"!

"The Vineyard" (40" x 40")

This was my very first attempt at a wholecloth quilt and shadow trapunto. It was machine quilted on my longarm quilting machine. I used a 100% cotton, batiste fabric as the quilt top. The backing is a glazed cotton. The green and pink effects came from bright, neon fabric placed between the layers of the quilt. I truly enjoyed this process. It stretched my creativity and I just love the results.
– Ellen Trojan, Waterside Quilting

*O*ne of the greatest things about shadow trapunto is the ability to hide the raw edges of the bright, neon fabric under the white trapunto. This gave Ellen the ability to change colors in her quilt. She has the raw edges of the pink and green fabric hidden under the rope stencil that is framing her centerpiece. Ellen also trimmed her batting away from all of the vines, leaves and grapes in her border. A difficult task! The trapunto batting in shadow trapunto needs to be very dense to produce opaque effects if you are using batiste or a sheer fabric. A thin, dense, poly batting such as "Quilters Dream Poly" is perfect for most shadow trapunto work. Binding fabric can be matched to the color your quilt gives you after quilting (see "Clover Valley" by author) or can be the original white fabric used in the quilt top. White binding gives the wall hanging a framed effect.

Appliqué & Pieced Quilts

*W*hen a customer gives me a pieced top to quilt, they usually say, "Please do whatever you want". This creative freedom is wonderful but I tend to go hog wild. I have a large supply of quilting stencils that I can audition. However, sometimes finding the right size can be a problem. When that happens I draw out original designs on paper. (Having an original design is always a plus.) I can erase my pencil marks on paper much more easily than if I were marking directly onto the quilt top. When I am finished with my design, I transfer it by sliding the artwork under the fabric and tracing the pattern with blue water-soluble pen onto the quilt top. For darker fabric, a light box is a useful tool for transferring the design.

Before I start to mark a quilt top, I have to know if all of the fabric has been washed. If it has not, it may bleed. This usually happens with hand-dyed or batik fabric. One small piece of batik fabric in an appliquéd quilt top can be a terrible surprise when I dunk the quilt to dissolve the water-soluble thread. If any of the fabric pieces are going to bleed in warm water, trapunto may not be a good option for the quilt. You can pick out the temporary stitches by hand but that would be extremely time-consuming. If you can not get the quilt top wet, you can still use a purple air-erase pen for marking.

I add trapunto whenever it would enhance the appliqué or plain space in a pieced quilt. When I see a quilt with a traditional pattern, like an Irish Chain quilt, I would immediately think that the quilt could use trapunto in the plain space to show off a beautiful feathered wreath. Trapunto is versatile, however, and can also be added to contemporary designs.

Designing, Marking, and Adding Trapunto to Pieced Tops

The fabrics of this unquilted appliqué top had been washed so I knew I could trapunto safely.

Here is a close-up of one of the appliqué blocks before trapunto or quilting.

I decided to draw some interesting designs in between the quilt blocks. I copied the pattern blocks out on paper first to get an idea of spacing.

*W*hen I completed my designs, I placed the drawings under the quilt and used a light box to trace them directly onto the fabric.

*R*ulers are useful for adding a quarter inch to the piecing and appliqué. You can enlist random teenagers to help you mark the quilt top. Sometimes the teenagers have interesting taste in nail polish. Not that there is anything wrong with blue finger nail polish…

*A*dding trapunto to the quarter inch motif will create the illusion of cording after the quilting is finished.

$\mathcal{W}$hen I am ready to start the first stages of trapunto, I load my batting onto my longarm quilting machine. Do not load the quilt backing at this time.

$\mathcal{N}$ext, pin the quilt top to the trapunto batting and load your machine with water-soluble thread and a poly or cotton bobbin thread that won't show through your quilt top after you get rid of your water-soluble products.

$\mathcal{A}$ large cone of "Vanish" water-soluble thread is excellent for the longarm quilter. This is a **warm** water-soluble product.

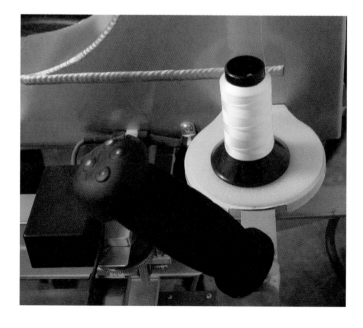

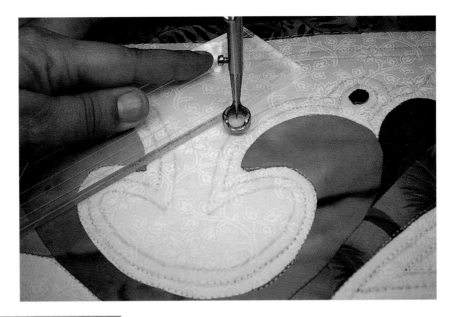

*C*arefully outline the appliqué and quilting designs with the water-soluble thread. This process holds the trapunto batting to the quilt top temporarily. You can use a straight edge to help control your foot.

*A*fter quilting all of the appliqué and other designs to your trapunto batting, the back of the quilt should look like this. It is now ready for the trapunto trimming process.

*H*ere is an example of the cutaway before the trapunto trimming is finished. The trapunto process takes longer and extra care is needed when there are tight spots to trim away.

When the trapunto is trimmed away the quilt can be loaded onto the quilt frame. The top will be slightly wavy until the final quilting is completed.

The quilting designs seem to be lost at this stage. The trapunto desperately needs heavy background fillers to push it into high relief.

Here's a close-up of an appliqué block after adding trapunto but before quilting the background fillers.

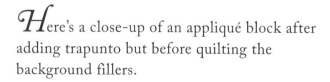

$\mathcal{L}$oad the quilt backing and the main batting and pin the quilt top to the layers. This quilt is now officially ready for quilting!

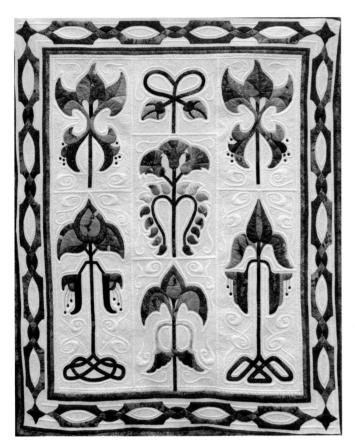

$\mathcal{A}$fter quilting the background fillers, the trapunto has a dense, sculptured feel. Its nicely packed appearance mimics the appliqué.

$\mathcal{H}$ere is a close-up of the appliqué block after adding trapunto and quilting the background fillers.

*T*hese extreme close-ups show the benefits of adding trapunto and heavy background fillers, such as McTavishing and stippling, to an appliqué quilt.

"*M*cTavishing", an alternative background filler, is as effective as stippling. It pushes down the background which allows the trapunto or appliqué designs to appear in high relief. This style of quilting creates movement and adds interest.

McTavishing

Water-soluable thread

*T*o begin "McTavishing," stitch in the ditch around the area you wish to quilt. Stitch a wave away from the ditch and then echo the wave back to the ditch. Use the ditch to move over a little bit and then echo the wave back to the point you pivoted on. Echo the wave back to the ditch and move over. After stitching about five wave lines, you are ready to move on to a new point and begin another wave series. Continue to create sections of wave lines, backtracking as little as possible. Use outer wave lines as the base for new sets of wave lines. See the "McTavishing" diagrams on page 184. For more detailed illustrations and instructions on "McTavishing" and other background fillers see *Quilting for Show*, by Karen McTavish.

Paper Designs for Pieced Tops

The piecing space can be challenging when designing a quilt top. When nothing in my stencil stash seems to work, I draw the piecing out on paper and create my own quilting designs.

Here is an example of my designs, drawn on paper, and then traced onto the fabric using a water-soluble blue pen. When the entire quilt is marked it is ready for trapunto.

This is the back of the quilt top. I've trimmed the extra batting away from the design and it is ready for quilting. I am using a low-loft batting, but it is very dense so it will do the trick.

I am showing curved trapunto designs in the plain yellow fabric and straight-line quilting in the busy fabrics.

*T*he trapunto is obvious and eye-catching after the markings and water-soluble thread are removed. This quilt is touring with American Professional Quilting Systems (APQS).

Here is another example of using paper when crafting a quilt top. I have traced the outline of the swag on paper so I can play around with design ideas in the empty spaces.

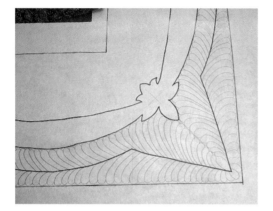

Draw your designs with a pencil first.

When you are happy with your paper design, re-draw your lines using a black, permanent ink marker for easy visibility.

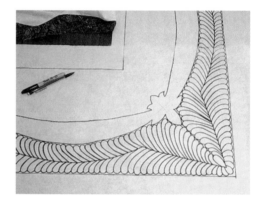

Now, place the paper drawing under the quilt, line up the corners, and trace the drawing onto your quilt top using a blue water-soluble pen.

The quilt designs have been quilted and the water-soluble products (thread and blue pen) have been soaked out. The quilt is ready for binding.

"Wholecloth/Trapunto #1" (37" x 41")

This original wholecloth was finished in 2002 after hosting Karen in my studio for several workshops. It was one of my class projects. I loved the process and have done more trapunto since then. Before becoming a longarm machine quilter, I taught quilt making, hand quilting and appliqué. When I was taking Karen's class I thought, "This is never going to work...I can't do that." But with Karen's patient assistance I did get it finished. I have since made another wholecloth trapunto quilt. It was a queen sized quilt, made for a four-poster bed. It took me approximately 96 hours to complete. When I gave it to my cousin at her wedding she and her husband were speechless. It was made especially for them with their initials in the center. The bridal wholecloth given to my cousin won the blue ribbon in a local quilt show.

- Joann "Jo" Stuebing, Jo's Quiltin' Quarters

$\mathcal{J}$oann hosted me in her studio for 4 days of classes. After I finished teaching classes for the day, the student/teacher roles would reverse. Joann, an accomplished appliqué quilter, would secretly sit me down and teach me how to appliqué. This was something I was dying to learn but a concept I didn't think I could wrap my brain around. She helped me start my very first appliqué block which now hangs in my studio, with its ugly flaws and scars, a lesson in humility. She hooked me to the needle-turn method and I haven't stopped doing appliqué since. Her wholecloth wall hanging uses the hand quilters' trick of using a darker value of thread color to give the design work a boost and become more noticeable. I understand she now offers trapunto as part of her quilting business. Joann has won many quilting awards for her amazing, traditional, appliqué hand work, machine trapunto and longarm machine quilting.

"Rose of Ella" (80" x 80")

I made this large, appliqué quilt for my niece, Ella Rose McTavish. She is my first niece and she is a wild child, hence the wild border, picked by Barb Engleking and approved by my mother. (As a predominantly traditional quilter, the border seemed quite contemporary to me.) I have noticed that adding trapunto to appliqué does very well in quilt shows and also that judges really like "McTavishing" as a background filler. I combined these techniques in this quilt. I think the "McTavishing" goes perfectly as a background to the appliqué. The most important thing, when you are deciding whether "to trapunto or not to trapunto," is to know if the fabrics have been washed. If they haven't been, they could bleed when you are soaking the quilt to remove the water-soluble thread. Since all the fabrics were washed first, I knew I could trapunto the appliqué. - *Karen McTavish*

"ALL KINDS -THE JOY OF SHARING" *(50" x 62")*

Judy Stingl Timm was willing to share a beautiful piece of poinsettia fabric, as well as the background fabric, so I could make this holiday version of "All Kinds." The pattern originally required set-in seams, but it has been updated eliminating the need for them, although precise piecing is still required to insure all the points meet. This pattern is featured in "More Quilts from the Quiltmakers Gift."
- Joanne Larsen Line
(Quilted by Karen McTavish)

*T*his quilt used trapunto to show off the quilting in the busy fabrics. As with many of Joanne's quilts, the fabrics were not pre-washed. When I submerged this quilt in water to remove the water-soluble thread, I noticed that the sashing fabric was starting to bleed into the white background fabrics. Panic set in as the white fabric started to look pink! Luckily, the bleed didn't have any staying power and Joanne was able to get the stain out. Trapunto with red fabrics - I should have known better!! You should always find out if your fabrics have been washed before you use trapunto. Whew!

"Windblown Square –Falling Leaves" (50" x 62")

Karen incorporated trapunto into this quilt which gives the appearance of three different layers of texture to the piecing design. She also quilted ropes and architectural scrollwork in the border. This quilt is featured in my book, "More Quilts from The Quiltmakers Gift." - **Joanne Larsen Line (Quilted by Karen McTavish)**

Joanne Line is our local "top-dog" quilter. She pieces so many quilts she needs a small army of machine quilters to help her finish them! Joanne is one of my favorite customers because she gives me complete creative freedom with her quilts. *Windblown Square* was a trapunto challenge. There was limited plain space for trapunto to be easily seen and I never like to overpower the pattern by quilting over the piecing lines. I did some contemporary trapunto using an architectural border stencil which I modified to make a matching center motif. The design was marked directly on the quilt using a ruler, chalk pencil, and two stencils.

"Fruits of My Labor" (88"x 88")

This was my first appliqué quilt. The pattern is from Piece O' Cake Designs and was taught as a block of the month class at Fabric Works in Superior, WI. After finishing the blocks, I wanted to set them in a different way, so my husband, Dale, designed the tree block in the center. Karen McTavish completed the trapunto and machine quilting. This quilt won a blue ribbon in 2002 in a national quilt show. This was my first blue ribbon for the traditional quilts category. The quilt now hangs in the lobby of "Relf Eye Associates." - **Diane Nyman (Quilted by Karen McTavish)**

*D*iane has been a quilting customer of mine since the first month I started quilting. She brings me her "special" quilts. As her machine quilter, this usually means "challenging." Quilts with beautiful appliqué and trapunto are the ones which do so well in quilt shows. This was my first thought when Diane brought me "Fruits of My Labor." Diane's appliqué fruits needed to pop out of the quilt, and I wanted the trapunto quilting designs to be a secondary feature in her quilt. Vase work, a popular quilting design, is repeated four times around the tree. "McTavishing" is used as background quilting around the appliqué to bring movement and interest to the blocks. The heavy quilting pushes the background fabric down, causing the appliqué to be the primary focus as it "pops" up. I added trapunto to the traditional cable and feather border stencil, which historically works well with the appliqué and fabrics. This is a national award-winning quilt.

"New England Stencil Quilt" (84" x 102")

*I have been quilting for about twenty years. My favorite form of quilting is hand appliqué using the needle-turn method. I started this quilt as a relief from an appliqué project that had many, very tiny pieces. I was excited about the larger appliqué pieces and the color palette this quilt had from the beginning. It is a traditional sampler block design with some reverse appliqué and embroidery. This quilt won two ribbons at a national quilt show recently. - **Marlyce Payne**
(Quilted by Karen McTavish)*

$\mathcal{M}$arlyce is an award-winning, appliqué quilter. She brings me mostly appliqué quilt tops, and gives me creative freedom to design the quilting for her piece. The borders became the most challenging and rewarding part of her quilt for me. Although both the swag and the fabrics are very traditional, the scallop shaped borders create white space which is difficult to design around. The space on one side of the swag is not equal in shape or size to the space on the other side. You can't throw the same quilting design around the scallops - you squeeze the designs in where you can. I designed the quilting border on paper first, and then transferred the drawing to the quilt top using a light box. The entire border was marked directly on the quilt before I loaded the quilt into my quilting machine. (See the "Paper Designs for Pieced Tops" section.) Trapunto was then introduced to the appliqué, swag border and quilting designs. Once the trimming was completed, I was ready to start to quilt. I used "McTavishing" as the background filler in the blocks to help create movement and add interest.

"Rachel's Garden" (74" x 94")

"Rachel's Garden" is a hand-appliquéd, Jacobean flower garden. This is an adapted version of Patricia Campbell's, "Romantica." My mother loved flowers. This garden is for her — with no weeds. The needle-turn appliqué was done with silk thread. The quilt has trapunto under all the appliqué, appliqué borders and the quilting stencil surrounding the border. - Patricia Ribich (Quilted by Karen McTavish)

When Pat's quilt arrived at my studio my first thoughts were, "Yes! White space! Trapunto!" I knew I would trapunto all the appliqué in the quilt but really struggled with a quilting stencil for the border. I finally made a custom design and drew it by hand onto the quilt top. I used a hill-and-valley style feather border on each side of the appliqué border. I also struggled with the decision of background fillers. This quilt used contemporary fabrics and design, so I knew I could incorporate both traditional and modern quilting techniques. "McTavishing" - a fun, somewhat unconventional, background filler - is used inside the borders of the quilting design. There are random, quilted feather scrolls all over the main portion of the quilt to add interest to the background stippling.

"OLD-FASHIONED SUNBONNETS" (42" x 60")

*When I first saw Betty Alderman's "Old-Fashioned Sunbonnets" offered as a block of the month project at my local quilt shop, I knew I had to do it. I really enjoyed doing each block as we moved through the seasons. Karen's creative quilting sets this quilt apart. This quilt received a "Viewers Choice" award in a state quilt show in 2002. – **Barb Sawdy (Quilted by Karen McTavish)***

*T*his is an interesting quilt in terms of quilting design decisions. Here was my dilemma: This quilt pattern is very conventional, and the fabrics, traditional. It has an American/country theme to it and historically, trapunto may not have been the right choice for this quilt. However, I really wanted to trapunto this quilt. I thought it would make the "Sue's" look great. But I know that judges can be very particular on historical accuracy. The end decision was to avoid trapunto and use traditional quilting in the border instead. I pushed the envelope and added "McTavishing" in each block as the background filler, quilting with a slightly darker, contrasting thread. The appliqué was stitched by machine, with the buttonhole stitch. The quilting in the sashing makes me feel comfortable that I did not cut any corners.

"Nesting in the Flowers" (88"x 93")

*This original, queen-size quilt was designed to coordinate with my son and daughter-in-law's wallpaper border in their bedroom. I looked at many quilts and quilting books for ideas and finally used my own to create this one-of-a-kind quilt. Color trapunto was introduced to fill up some of the white space. This quilt is a national, multiple award-winner. - **Pat Sowada***
(Quilted by Karen McTavish)

When I received Pat's quilt I was excited to see that it was full of plain space. It needed great quilting. But what would work? I called Pat and asked if she could send drawings of her original appliqué design. When they arrived, I knew I could convert Pat's appliqué designs to quilting designs to enhance her quilt. I also measured the tan "on-point" blocks and made my own paper design to fit that space. (This design is now a popular stencil called "McScrollwork" and is available on my website.) This quilt is successful in show because of its original appliqué and quilting designs and its unusual, color-trapunto batting.

"My First Quilt" (102" x 102")

I've titled this quilt "My First Quilt" since it was my first quilting project. I used the block of the month patterns "Through Grandmother's Window", by Piece O' Cake Designs. I decided to appliqué the flowers in shades of purple to remind me of the poem, "When I Grow Old I Shall Wear Purple." These colors speak to my age. The quilt was sent to Karen to quilt and trapunto. Karen asked me to enter this quilt in a national quilt show where "My First Quilt" won Best of Show – Longarm.
- Ruth Sundby (Quilted by Karen C. McTavish)

*L*ife is just not fair. How is it possible to enter your very first appliqué quilt in a quilt show and win one of the "Best of Show" awards? This would never happen to my first quilt, that's for sure! Ruth gave me creative freedom when she handed me her quilt and told me to do "whatever." I pretended to know what I was doing but when she left my studio I just about cried from fear. Ruth used batiks, which are modern fabrics, so I knew I could risk "going contemporary." I decided to "McTavish" the backgrounds of each block and I continued this design into the sashing as it seemed too wide to leave un-quilted. I discovered that the quilts that scare me the most creatively, are quilts that turn into my very best work! One of the critiques we received from a quilt judge wrote this comment about Ruth's quilt: "Machine quilter appears to be having way too much fun quilting this quilt."

Diagrams of "McTavishing"

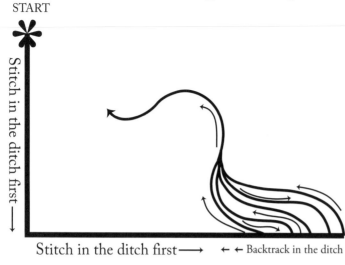

START

Stitch in the ditch first →

Stitch in the ditch first → ← ← Backtrack in the ditch

STEP 1:

Stitch in the ditch around the area you will be "McTavishing." Then starting anywhere on the ditch, stitch a wave away from the ditch and echo the wave back to the ditch. Use the ditch to move over to another spot to echo the wave back to the point you pivoted on. After about five wavy lines of stiching you are ready to move on to a new spot.

STEP 2:

Move on to a new point from which you will begin the new series of wavy lines.

START

Stitch in the ditch first →

Stitch in the ditch first → ← ← Backtrack in the ditch

START

Stitch in the ditch first →

Stitch in the ditch first → ← ← Backtrack in the ditch

STEP 3:

Continue to create areas of wavy lines, backtracking as little as possible. Use outer wave lines as the base for new sets of wavy lines as shown.

Resources

Book Sources

Brightbill, Dorothy. <u>Quilting as a Hobby</u>. New York, NY: Bonanza Books/Crown Publishers, 1963

Cabanel, André-Jean. <u>Piqué de Provence.</u> Aix-en-Provence, France: Sarl Édisud, 2000

Colby, Averil. <u>Quilting</u>. New York: Charles Scribner's Sons, 1971

Cory, Pepper. <u>Mastering Quilt Marking</u>. Lafayette, CA: C&T Publishing, 1999

Fons, Marianne. <u>Fine Feathers</u>. Lafayette, CA: C&T Publishing, 1988

Gaudynski, Diane. <u>Guide to Machine Quilting</u>. Paducah, KY: American Quilters Society, 2002

Halgrimson, Jan and Shirley Thompson. <u>Quilts - Start to Finish</u>. Vancouver, WA: Powell Publications 1997.

McTavish, Karen C. <u>Quilting for Show</u>. Duluth, MN: Karen McTavish, 2002

Morgan, Mary and Dee Mosteller. <u>Trapunto and Other Forms of Raised Quilting</u>. New York: Charles Scribner's Sons, 1923

Newman, Thelma R. <u>Quilting, Patchwork, Appliqué, and Trapunto</u>. New York, New York: Crown Publishers, 1974

Orlofsky, Patsy and Myron. <u>Quilts in America</u>. New York: McGraw-Hill Book Company, 1974

Rodgers, Sue H. <u>Trapunto: The Handbook of Stuffed Quilting</u>. Wheat Ridge, CO: Leman Publications, 1990

Safford, Carleton L. and Robert Bishop. <u>America's Quilts and Coverlets</u>. New York, New York: Weathervane Books/Barre Publishing, 1974

Shaw, Robert. <u>Quilts: A Living Tradition</u>. Shelburne, Vermont: Hugh Lauter Levin Associates, Inc./Beaux Arts Editions, 1995

Squire, Helen. <u>Helen's Guide to Quilting in the 21st Century</u>. Paducah, KY: AQS, 1996. <u>Dear Helen Can You Tell Me?...All About Quilting Designs</u>. Paducah, KY: American Quilter's Society, 1987

Walner, Hari. <u>Trapunto by Machine</u>. Lafayette, CA: C&T Publishing, 1996. <u>Exploring Machine Trapunto – New Dimensions</u>. Lafayette, CA: C&T Publishing, 1999

Webster, Marie D. <u>Quilts – Their Story and How to Make Them</u>. Garden City, New York: Doubleday, Doran and Company Inc., 1928

Pattern Sources

Betty Alderman Designs
PO Box 409, Palmyra, NY 14522

Letterbox Quilts Block of the Month
www.LetterboxQuilts.com

Patricia B. Campbell
www.patcampbell.com

Piece O' Cake Designs
Becky Goldsmith and Linda Jenkins
<u>The Appliqué Sampler</u>. Available through C&T Publishing or www.pieceocake.com

Quilt Nouveau Designs
www.quiltnouveau.com

Internet Sources

http://www.bidwellhousemuseum.org/Collections/Quilt_documentation_2.htm

http://www.museum.state.il.us/muslink/art/htmls/ks_whole.html

http://www.plainandsimplequilts.com/whole%20cloth.htm

http://www.osv.org/pages/Warmth_Display.html

http://www.sewbaby.com

http://www.womenfolk.com/historyofquilts/wholecloth.htm

Photography Sources and Sites

Jeff Frey & Associates Photography Inc.
405 East Superior Street
Duluth, MN 55802
phone: 218-722-6630
fax: 218-722-8452

The Fairlawn Mansion and Museum
906 East Second Street
Superior, WI 54880
715-394-5712
www.fairlawnmansion.org

Mathew S. Burrows 1890 Inn
1632 East First Street
Duluth, MN 55812
218-724-4991
800-789-1890
www.visitduluth.com/1890inn

The New Scenic Café
5461 North Shore Drive
Duluth, MN 55804
218-525-6274
www.sceniccafe.com

Contributing Quilters

Theodosia (Teddy) Wicktor Ahern
11 Colonial Drive
Penfield, NY 14526
(585) 381-4987
theodosi@rochester.rr.com

Linda J. Alexander
Oregon Machine Quilting Company
5833 NW Highland Place / Corvallis, OR
97330 (541) 745-9081
Linda@oregonquilting.com
www.oregonquilting.com

Melanie Austin
Huckleberry Stitches Custom Machine
Quilting
2811 Sharon Drive / Post Falls, ID 83854
(208) 773-1048
tmaustin@peoplepc.com

Jill L. Bennett
Quilter with a View
P.O. Box 1043 / Ward Cove, Alaska 99928
(907) 225-0934
jbennett@kpunet.net

Kathryn Blais
Quilted Treasures
5-1 Victoria Drive / Auburn, MA 01501
(508) 832-8355
katquilts@charter.net

Mary A. Bojan
Flying Needle Custom Machine Quilting
1063 Sandstone Ct. / Aurora, IL 60504
(630) 898-7267
flyinneedle@aol.com

Marcia J. Bowen
214 Maple Road
Barrington, IL 60010
(847) 381-1597
sequinsmb@aol.com

Kim Brunner
Goose the Moose Quilting
19826 Burlington Path / Farmington, MN
55024 (651) 463-6705
kimmyquilt@aol.com

Janiece Cline
Piece by Piece Quilting
8316 Allman Road / Lenexa, KS 66219
(913) 894-2702
piece_by_piece_quilting@hotmail.com
www.PiecebyPieceQuilting.com

Carole Denny-Oelrich
Eagle's Nest Quilting Studio
951 Canyonville-Riddle Road / Riddle, OR
97469 (541) 839-4100 (541) 863-2872
keneu@frontiernet.net

Sherri Dolly
Scrap Basket Quilting
11811 W. 99th Terrace / Overland Park, KS
66214 (913) 438-4226 (Phone)
(913) 541-8386 (Fax)
scrapbasket@kc.rr.com

Winnie Haley
Winnies Quilting
4248 Bayshore Circle / Granbury, TX 76049
(817) 326-3122
winrichly@yahoo.com

Shireen Hattan
Shireenz Stitchez
70051 W. Meadow Parkway / Sisters, OR
97759 (541) 549-1181
shireen@bendcable.com

Contributing Quilters

Monty Sue Haubold
Monty's Flying Needle
P.O. Box 423 / New Lebanon, NY 12125
(518) 794-7884
montyquilts@cs.com

Carol Hilton
Southern Heritage Quilting
19666 Hoo Shoo Too Road / Baton Rouge,
LA 70817 (225) 753-1882
SHQuilting@aol.com

Jacqueline M. Kamlet
Painting with Stitches
36 Porter Drive / West Hartford, CT 06117
(860) 965-9512 jkamlet@attbi.com
www.PaintingWithStitches.com

Kathy Knox
Quilting Memories by Kathy
1000 Aspen Blvd. /Brandon, SD
57005 (605) 582-2614
knoxkath@splitrocktel.net

Joanne Larsen Line
Author, Quilting Instructor, Mentor
2008 Swan Lake Rd. / Duluth, MN 55811
(218) 727-1390 / (218) 722-4434 (fax)
jline@d.umn.edu

Aurora Lowell
MooseQuilteers
6755 Beech Court / Arvada, CO 80004
(720) 898-5299
alowell@townsend.com

Becky Manske
Becky's Custom Quilting
2936 Saturn Avenue / Eau Claire, WI
54703 (715) 834-8386
manskeb@hotmail.com

Jan McTavish
1764 Wildwood Rd .
 Duluth, MN 55804
(218) 525-0103
janmctavish@hotmail,com

Michelle Miller
The Quilter's Cabin
49684 440th Street / Perham, MN 56573
(218) 346-6261
dmmillers@arvig.net

Debra S. Murphy
One Stitch at a Time Quilting
1470 48th Street / Marion, IA 52302
(319) 373-4106
detour4me@aol.com

Diane Nyman
3344 Lindahl Road
Duluth, MN 55810
(218) 624-0260
quilter.man@prodigy.net

Christine M. Olson
Cascade Custom Quilting
P.O. Box 1662 / Buckley, WA 98321
(253) 891-8543 hotquilts@hotmail.com
www.cascadecustomquilting.com

Marlyce Payne
7316 Niagara Lane North
Maple Grove, MN 55311
(763) 494-3479
empayne@unique-software.com

Betty Peine
Sweet Dreams Machine Quilting
370 North Fairway Drive E. / Hoodsport,
WA 98548 (360) 877-6842
quilting@hctc.com cbpeine@hctc.com

Janice E. Petre
Janice Petre's House of Quilting
200 Gelsinger Road / Sinking Spring, PA
19608 (610) 678-7976
jphoq@yahoo.com

Sandra D. Reed
Creative Machine Quilting
115 Crawford Rose Dr./ Aurora, Ontario,
Canada L4G 4S1 (905) 727-1707
davis@neptune.on.ca

Marcia Rhone
Clear Pond Quilting
E 6803 White Lake Road / Weyauwega,
WI 54983 (920) 867-3426
mrhone@wolfnet.net

Patricia Ribich
308 6th Avenue North
Sauk Rapids, NB 56379
(320) 255-5448
ribichpe@aol.com

Contributing Quilters

Cathy Rogers
Cherry Hill Quilter
134 Barcroft Drive / Cherry Hill, NJ
08034 (856) 216-7597
chquilter@comcast.net

Sherry D. Rogers
Runway Ranch Longarm Quilting Services
19702 8th Avenue South / Des Moines, WA
98148 (206) 878-4720
sewfarsewgood@msn.com
www.sewfaresewgood.org

Barb Sawdy
13132 Walnut Drive
Burnsville, MN 55337
(952) 895-1945
bsawdy@juno.com

Susan Schmieden
The Quilting Connection
21 Adams Street / Elkhorn, WI 53121
(262) 723-6775
www.longarmconnection.com

Carol A. Selepec
Create A Stitch
17 Seventh Street / Midland, PA 15059
(724) 643-4833
createastitch@access995.com

Beverly Sievers
Dancing Threads Heirloom Machine Quilting
184 Gray Street / Elk Run Heights, IA
50707 (319) 236-2279
dancingthreads@mchsi.com
www.dancingthreads.com

Kathy J. Slater
Stems & Stitches
6711 West 200 South / South Whitley, IN
46787 (260) 723-4345
stemsandstitches@kconline.com

Pat Sowada
1675 Golden Spike Road
Sauk Rapids MN 56379
(320) 251-7029

Kim Stotsenberg
Sew-N-Sew Quilting
10314 Bethel Burley Road / Port Orchard,
WA 98367 (360) 876-3116
Thatsewnsew@aol.com

Joann "Jo" Stuebing
Jo's Quiltin' Quarters
534 S.W. Antique Lane / Grants Pass, OR
(541) 476-8522
jqquartr@msn.com

Ruth Sundby
2541 14 ½ Avenue SE
St. Cloud, MN 56304
(320) 252-0847
sundby@astound.net

Barbara R. Tibus
Quilts to Treasure
886 Shoemaker Avenue / West Wyoming,
PA 18644 (570) 693-0507
btibus@adelphia.net

Ellen Trojan
Waterside Quilting
7075 Driftwood Dr. / Fenton, MI 48430
(810) 629-8095
artrojan@aol.com

Janice L. Walsh
Cats' Meow Quilting
13425 Lisbon Road / Brookfield, WI 53005
(262) 781-3646 pumapdw@execpc.com
pumapdw@yahoo.com

Marsha West
Forgotten Arts
9565 Owasso Road / Fowlerville, MI 48836
(517) 223-7992
marsha8181@earthlink.net

Acknowledgements

This book was not written alone. My starting point has always been my mother, Jan McTavish; encouraging me, believing in me, introducing me to quilting, and supporting me along the way. She has helped me immeasurably with the development of this book with suggestions, reviews, reactions, and the occasional quilting retreat. She has spent a considerable amount of time contributing and adding original concepts to this project. I am so thankful to her for her artistic quilting standards and for inviting me to share her passion.

I also had an enormous amount of help and support from the rest of my wonderful family, who I love very much, but more importantly – they love me. I honor my family and friends and am indebted to them for everything I have in my life. Without their support I would not have had the courage to be a self-employed single mom.

Thank you to the publishers, Sara Duke and David Devere of On-Word Bound Books. They believed in me and in the creation of this book. Their commitment and dedication to this project was monumental. This book was a huge part of their life and without their help, vision, and support this book would have never seen the light of day. I want to thank them for all their work including the stunning location shots, which were taken in various settings around our lovely town of Duluth, Minnesota.

Thank you to all the longarm machine quilters, students, my quilting customers and longarm colleagues for allowing me to use their masterpieces in this book. Without your fabulous beauties, it wouldn't have been much of a book to look at.

I want to give a special thanks to Steve Tiggman from Jeff Frye & Associates of Duluth, MN for photographing the featured quilts. Shooting whitework is a challenge for the most adept photographer but he was able to capture the subtle beauty of these quilts with professional ease.

Thank-you to Jahn Opheim, Curator of Education, at The Fairlawn Mansion and Museum, who opened up a time in her day to allow us to display quilts throughout the historic exhibits.

A big thank-you to Alan Fink, the proprietor of The Matthew S. Burrow's 1890's Inn Bed and Breakfast, who graciously gave us free reign in his establishment to move furniture, remake the beds, and cause general chaos with our pile of quilts.

To Rita B and and Scott at The New Scenic Café, thank you for generously sharing your beautiful gardens on multiple days as we strove for a mix of good weather and perfect blooms.

I would also like to thank the following people who have given me inspiration throughout my life: Sherry D. Rogers, Cheryl Dennison, Barb Engelking, Joanne Larsen Line, Helen Smith Stone, and Northern Lights Machine Quilters Guild.

Thank-you to the women who allowed the likeness of their patterns to be printed in this book: Helen Squire, Patricia Campbell, Betty Alderman, and the Piece O' Cake ladies – Becky Goldsmith and Linda Jenkins.

I would like to extend an additional thank-you to Letterbox Quilts – Block of the Month and Binky Brown Takahashi, Quilt Nouveau Designs, pattern designer of "Garden Glories" - the pieced quilt in the "Adding Trapunto to Pieced Quilts" section.

Glossary

Auditioning - A term I use when I am planning a design for my wholecloth using stencils. I try out different stencils, ideas, and designs until I make up my mind.

Batting - A layer sandwiched inside the quilt between the top and the backing; usually made of a polyester, cotton or wool blend which adds warmth, loft and texture to a quilt.

Binding - A doubled strip of fabric, cut on the either the straight of grain or the bias. It is stitched to the edge of the quilt to cover the raw edges of the quilt top, batting, and backing.

Bleeding - When bright colored fabric or hand-dyed batting comes in contact with warm water it can release some of its dye and stain the quilt top.

Color Trapunto - This trapunto technique uses neon colored acrylic felt for the trapunto batting with a sheer fabric quilt top.

Longarm Machine Quilting – Generally, a hand-guided, quilting machine which has a large industrial throat (longarm) that provides a fast, high quality and effective way to stitch a quilt together in a functional and decorative manner. A list of longarm machine quilters can be found in this book.

McTavishing - A quilting background filler used in machine quilting. This term came from my fellow longarm machine quilters. They saw my work on my website - www.designerquilts.com and commented that my style of background filler should be called "McTavishing." It stuck like glue. This is a heavy background filler, a contemporary alternative to tight stippling. I like to think of this filler as "Wonder Woman Comic Book Style Hair," but that doesn't roll off the tongue easily.

Meandering - A medium to large sized quilting design which looks like jigsaw puzzle pieces. It "wanders" around the quilt top, holding the layers together.

Micro Stippling – Blindingly-tiny stipple designs; the path can barely be seen with the naked eye. It is achieved using a magnifying glass which is attached to the head of the quilting machine.

Plainspace - An area in a wholecloth quilt without motifs or designs. Background fillers such as crosshatching or straight-line quilting can be used here.

Registration Lines - A term I use for the first stage of wholecloth design. Registration lines are a placement guideline needed to create a wholecloth. They are crucial to the stencil auditioning process. These lines are not to be quilted.

Shadow Trapunto - This trapunto technique uses a sheer fabric quilt top, regular trapunto batting, and a neon-bright piece of fabric placed between the layers of the trapunto and main batting. This trapunto technique gives the appearance of a dyed batting.

Squaring-Up - Cutting the wholecloth so it will hang straight and flat if on display or hanging from a sleeve on rod and drape.

Stippling - A very small, jigsaw-puzzle style meandering design and background filler. This pushes the fabric into the background so other quilting designs or appliqué can show up in high relief.

Trapunto - A style of quilting which creates high relief quilting designs. Today, water-soluble thread and acrylic felt are incorporated into this technique instead of insertion of cotton or yarn through the backing.

Trapunto scissors - A sharp pair of scissors of your choice. They will be used for many hours of trimming trapunto batting. They must fit comfortably on the thumb and be very sharp to snip cleanly through the batting - generally not appliqué or duckbill scissors.

Whitework - A traditional term used for a white wholecloth quilt. Areas, spaces, or plain blocks which are in need of beautiful quilting motifs.

Wholecloth - A quilt made of one piece of cloth, generally not pieced together. The backing traditionally came from the same bolt of fabric as the top. Traditional wholecloth colors are white, off-white, and yellow.

Index

About the Author

*L*ongarm machine quilting allows Karen to combine her two passions: Wholecloth and Trapunto. Karen specializes in crafting award-winning quilts using techniques which allow machine quilters to replicate traditional "hand-quilted" effects. She has been featured on PBS's *Quilt Central,* and HGTV's *Simply Quilts.* Her work has appeared in Joanne Line's books, *Quilts from the Quilt Makers Gift #1* and *#2,* and numerous national magazines and journals. Karen's first book, *Quilting for Show,* was published in 2002. She has been a full time professional longarm quilter since 1997 - supporting herself and her daughter through her craft. Karen lives on Lake Superior's North Shore, quilting and teaching from her studio, throughout the country and in Canada. Contact her at 1748 Wildwood Road / Duluth, MN 55804 / (218) 525-0017 phone or (218) 525-1057 (fax) or visit her website at www.designerquilts.com